"The book inspires the pursuit of intellectual virtue—it makes attractive a life characterized by the traits Dow discusses. I wanted to renew my efforts in the direction of intellectual virtue having read it. And I know my students, many of whom enter college with no real aim in sight beyond a degree which promises a high-paying position, would benefit from such inspiration. . . . I can easily imagine using it for an orientation course we offer to freshman philosophy majors."

Gregg Ten Elshof, Biola University

"Here is a book that is greatly needed in the contemporary world. Moral failure is revealed daily in the media. Philip Dow demonstrates that moral failure is the result of defective intellectual character. I wish this book could be taught in every school in the world and read by every parent."

Gary Chapman, author of *The Five Love Languages* and *Love as a Way of Life*

"It is far easier to be conformed than it is to be transformed. Dow's book is a wake-up call for all of us to be diligent gardeners of our minds and souls."

Philip Walker, president of International Christian Ministries

"As I read Dow's book, I was struck with what a fresh and potent addition it would make to a college or high school course on critical thinking. It would do four things seldom emphasized in such a course: show in considerable detail how being a good thinker is a matter of one's character, show that getting such character is a matter of discipline, show a rich variety of motives for turning oneself into a good thinker, and provide substantial advice about the implementation of such discipline. The book has an easy, conversational style and is chock-full of vivid, discussable illustrations."

Robert C. Roberts, Baylor University

"*Virtuous Minds* is beautifully written with poise, balance and substance, hitting a number of nails very firmly on the head."

Julian Hardyman, senior pastor of Eden Baptist Church, Cambridge, UK

"Phil Dow has written a provocative, compelling and engaging book that challenges Christians to consider the importance of intellectual character and to encourage them to self-consciously nurture virtuous intellectual habits. The book is a delightful read that addresses a subject that needs careful intellectual inquiry. I would recommend this book to anyone who is intentional about growing spiritually or who is involved in the cultivation of spiritual formation in the lives of young people."

Daniel Egeler, vice president of Association of Christian Schools International and author of *Mentoring Millenials*

"Philip Dow has given us a really important book, one that is both motivating and a pleasure to read. With excellent illustrations and carefully reasoned arguments, Dow challenges us to examine the way we use our minds. We are confronted with the critical importance of intellectual courage, curiosity, honesty and humility, and we are reminded that the weeds of intellectual carelessness grow effortlessly and bring with them consequences that can be sobering. Although there are other books which address the subject of the Christian mind, I am aware of none that addresses this subject with the clarity, thoroughness or motivational quality of Dow's work."

Mike Treneer, president, The Navigators International

"While the Aristotle-inspired pursuit of the good life has generated an enormous literature on moral character, its importance and its development, the other side of the person, intellectual character, has been astonishingly neglected by both academics and (more importantly) the general public. Yet excellence, or 'virtue,' in both components is essential for leading the best kinds of life open to humans; fine traits of heart alone, without fine traits of mind, cannot get the job done. It is high time that explicit attention was paid—by educators, by parents, by leaders, by all of us—to the habits of mind that help people grab hold of truth, and to what it takes to develop such habits. *Virtuous Minds* is to be applauded for prompting such attention, and in such an accessible and practical-minded way. May it find the readership it deserves!"

Lawrence Lengbeyer, United States Naval Academy

Philip E. Dow

VIRTUOUS MINDS

Intellectual Character Development

courage

carefulness

tenacity

fairmindedness

curiosity

honesty

humility

**FOR
STUDENTS,
EDUCATORS
& PARENTS**

IVP Academic
An imprint of InterVarsity Press
Downers Grove, Illinois

InterVarsity Press
P.O. Box 1400, Downers Grove, IL 60515-1426
World Wide Web: www.ivpress.com
E-mail: email@ivpress.com

InterVarsity Press® is the book-publishing division of InterVarsity Christian Fellowship/USA®, a movement of students and faculty active on campus at hundreds of universities, colleges and schools of nursing in the United States of America, and a member movement of the International Fellowship of Evangelical Students. For information about local and regional activities, write Public Relations Dept., InterVarsity Christian Fellowship/USA, 6400 Schroeder Rd., P.O. Box 7895, Madison, WI 53707-7895, or visit the IVCF website at <www.intervarsity.org>.

All Scripture quotations, unless otherwise indicated, are taken from THE HOLY BIBLE, NEW INTERNATIONAL VERSION®, NIV® Copyright © 1973, 1978, 1984, 2011 by Biblica, Inc.™ Used by permission. All rights reserved worldwide.

While all stories in this book are true, some names and identifying information in this book have been changed to protect the privacy of the individuals involved.

Cover Design: Cindy Kiple
Images: ©Benjamin Howell/iStockphoto
Interior Design: Beth Hagenberg

ISBN 978-0-8308-2714-5

Printed in the United States of America ∞

Library of Congress Cataloging-in-Publication Data
Dow, Phil, 1970-
 Virtuous minds : intellectual character development / Philip E. Dow.
  pages cm
 Includes bibliographical references and index.
 ISBN 978-0-8308-2714-5 (pbk. : alk. paper)
 1. Character. 2. Personality development. 3. Education—Philosophy. I. Title.
BJ1521.D67 2013
241'.4—dc23

                                                                    2013001570

P	20	19	18	17	16	15	14	13	12	11	10	9	8	7	6
Y	30	29	28	27	26	25	24	23	22	21	20	19	18	17	

To the students, families, teachers,
staff and administrators of
Rosslyn Academy (Nairobi, Kenya)
and
The Bear Creek School (Redmond, Washington)

CONTENTS

ACKNOWLEDGMENTS

THE WRITING OF THIS LITTLE BOOK was very much a group effort. At the very top of the list is Dr. Jason Baehr, my very good friend and the person who not only introduced me to the concept of intellectual virtue but has been a model of these virtues as we have discussed them over the years. For those who want to explore intellectual character on a more philosophical level, there is no better place to start than Jason's recent book, *The Inquiring Mind* (Oxford University Press).

The second group that needs to be acknowledged is my family—especially my wife, Catherine, and my parents, Stewart and Elaine Dow, each of whom read all or most of this manuscript and provided important feedback, encouragement and support as the project slowly grew into a manuscript. Of course my daughters, Emma (who makes a cameo appearance) and Sophie, also deserve special mention as reservoirs of inspiration and joy to their daddy as he plodded along from one draft to another. Thanks also go to my sisters, Christy and Kathy, and to the Hoke boys (Brian, Sean and Stuart) for being such a wonderful source of joy to me. Finally, thank you to the Maidment clan as a whole, for welcoming me into their family.

My students at the Bear Creek School and Rosslyn Academy were the guinea pigs for many of the ideas in this book. As we talked about intellectual character, it was their creative thinking that forced me to consider our thinking habits in new and helpful ways. My desire to explain intellectual character to them in a clear and, perhaps even occasionally, inspiring way led me to the research that produced many of the anecdotes in this book.

My friends and colleagues during my years at the Bear Creek School, at Rosslyn Academy and now at Cambridge have also played an important role as models of intellectual character and important sources of encouragement or critical feedback. An exhaustive list of individuals in this group would fill several pages, but a few deserve special mention. They are the Venerable Society of Bede, the Committee, Andrew Preston, Rosslyn Football Club and the members of the Ashworth Estate.

Several other people were kind enough to read through drafts of the book and offered critiques that have made the book much better than it would have otherwise been. This group includes Jason Baehr, Dick Brogden, Patrick Caruth, Donna Dunn, Julian Hardyman, Brent Hanson, Don Mercer, Bob Roberts, the faculty of Rosslyn Academy, Kirsten Krymusa, Philip Walker and Jay Wood. I also need to express my sincere thanks to the fine editorial team at IVP for all their work in smoothing out the rough edges that existed in the original drafts of this book. Finally, several prominent authors need to be specifically acknowledged as having a major influence on this book through their writings. Some of them are quoted directly, while the influence of the others simply permeates the book as a whole. They are Jason Baehr, G. K. Chesterton, Andreas J. Köstenberger, C. S. Lewis, George Marsden, Alister McGrath, J. P. Moreland, Mark Noll, Ron Ritchhart, Robert Roberts, James Sire, Dallas Willard and Jay Wood.

FOREWORD

THIS BOOK IS THE FIRST OF ITS KIND and one that is urgently needed inside and outside the Christian community. Its subject matter is intellectual character. Typically, when we think of character, we are thinking of *moral* character, for example, of qualities like kindness, compassion and generosity. But the realm of personal character is not exhausted by the realm of moral character. It also has an *intellectual* dimension.

Your intellectual character consists of your inner attitudes and dispositions toward things like truth, knowledge and understanding. To get some idea of the quality of your intellectual character, consider the following questions: Do you care about learning and knowledge? Do you desire to understand the world around you? Are you curious about why things are the way they are, about the unfolding of history, and about what ultimately exists or what is ultimately good? Or, on the contrary, do you have a dim view of truth and knowledge? Or do you, perhaps, value knowledge and learning but only as a means to other ends, for example, to getting a job or impressing your friends? Are you indifferent to, or positively bored by, concepts like knowledge, truth and understanding?

Your answers to these questions say something important about the quality of your intellectual character. This is because good or "virtuous" intellectual character is marked, first and foremost, by a deep and abiding love of truth, a desire to know and understand things as they really are. Virtuous intellectual character also involves a number of other traits that arise from a love of truth, including inquisitiveness, attentiveness, intellectual carefulness and thoroughness, fair-mindedness, open-mindedness, intellectual courage, caution, tenacity and rigor. These traits are called "intellectual virtues." By contrast, bad or defective intellectual character is marked by a lack of concern with, or a positive disregard for, knowledge and truth and, more specifically, by traits such as intellectual laziness, carelessness, superficiality, narrow-mindedness, dishonesty and cowardice. These are known as "intellectual vices."

Theologians and philosophers have long been concerned with moral virtues such as those mentioned above and with theological virtues such as faith, hope and love. There are great and venerable treatises on these topics that date all the way back to the ancient Greek and early medieval periods. Surprisingly, however, these thinkers have had relatively little to say about the *intellectual* virtues—about the intellectual or cognitive dimension of personal character. This neglect of intellectual virtue at the scholarly level has had substantial and unfortunate consequences at the popular level. It has left the average person without the vocabulary or conceptual resources even to understand what virtuous intellectual character *is,* let alone to focus on it in a way that might actually lead to its realization. It has also left those outside the ivory tower (and many within it) unable to comprehend and evaluate significant events or persons around them. We have a hard time, for instance, understanding how a really smart scientist might perpetrate a major intellectual hoax. Or how a well-intentioned or morally upright person might misuse or ignore important evidence. In the first case, we fail to see that remarkable intelligence and impressive academic credentials are no guarantee that a person will actually care about truth—or, at least, care about it more than other values such as money, power and professional prestige. In the second case, we fail to see that a person might care sincerely about certain moral values such as freedom or justice while failing to give sufficient respect to the value of truth. In either case, the defects in question are defects of intellectual character.

Surely this academic and popular neglect of matters of intellectual character is a regrettable state of affairs—particularly when viewed from a Christian standpoint. While this seems obvious to me, and possibly to you, I shall briefly enumerate four reasons why Christians in particular should care about and give special attention to the intellectual dimension of personal character.

First, the Jewish and Christian Scriptures place a premium on a concern with or desire for truth. As the psalmist proclaims: "Yet you desired faithfulness even in the womb; you taught me wisdom in that secret place" (Psalm 51:6). This theme is spread throughout the Scriptures: for instance, in the call to treat "understanding" and "wisdom" like "silver" and to "search for it as for hidden treasure" (Proverbs 2:1-5); or in the apostle Paul's high regard for the Christians in Berea, who "received the message with great eagerness and examined the Scriptures every day to see if what Paul said was true" (Acts 17:11); or in his admonition to the church in Thessalonica not to "treat prophecies with contempt," but to "test them all" and "hold on to what is good" (1 Thessalonians 5:20-21); or in Jesus' statement that he *is* the truth (John 14:6). As noted above, a concern with truth is the very heart of virtuous intellectual character; it is what gives rise to the range of individual intellectual virtues such as reflectiveness, attentiveness, fair-mindedness, intellectual carefulness and courage.

But should Christians really care about knowledge or truth *in general*? Or should they, perhaps, care merely about biblical or theological knowledge? In this connection, it is often pointed out, correctly, that God has given to humanity two books: the inspired

Jewish and Christian Scriptures and the "book of nature." To care about knowledge in general—including the subject matter of history, mathematics, economics, psychology, philosophy and the like—is to care about the content of this second book. Similarly, it is often said that "all truth is God's truth," meaning that God and God alone is the ultimate source of all that is. If this is right, then Christians need not limit themselves to biblical or theological knowledge. For in doing so, they cut themselves off from a deeper and more profound understanding of the creation and its Creator.

Second, consider Jesus' graphic and startling condemnation of the Pharisees: "Woe to you, teachers of the law and Pharisees, you hypocrites! You are like whitewashed tombs, which look beautiful on the outside but on the inside are full of the bones of the dead and everything unclean" (Matthew 23:27). The implication is that to be truly good, to follow Jesus and his Father in the manner they intend, is to be transformed *from the inside out*. Mere external obedience—of which the Pharisees were masters—is woefully inadequate. What is it, then, to be transformed from the inside out? This depends in part on what we are like on the inside, that is, on the actual content of human nature and psychology. Clearly, part of who we are on the inside consists of our attitudes, feelings, motivations, beliefs and thinking *as they relate to* things like knowledge, truth and understanding. Assuming the latter are genuine values in God's eyes, then to the extent that we fail to care about truth or knowledge, we remain immature or defective as human beings. Put another way, part of Christian transformation is transformation of the intellectual dimension of personal character, that is, of our attitudes, motivations and feelings about truth, knowledge and related cognitive values. This is reminiscent of Paul's admonition to the Christians in Rome to be "transformed by the renewing of your mind. Then you will be able to test and approve what God's will is—his good, pleasing and perfect will" (Romans 12:2).

Third, one of the great and daunting commands of Jesus is to love our neighbors—including even our *enemies*—as ourselves. But what exactly does this require? What sorts of things must we actually *do* if we are to follow this command? My suggestion is that part of loving our neighbors and enemies as ourselves is exercising a range of intellectual virtues in our interactions with them. If I feed and clothe my neighbor but distort, belittle or otherwise disrespect his beliefs, then surely I fail to love him as Christ commands. This is a reflection of the fact that our beliefs are an important part of *who we are,* such that to have them ignored, caricatured, disregarded or the like is to feel ignored, caricatured or disregarded ourselves. Accordingly, part of the radical love to which Christ calls us is a consistent exercise, in our interactions with others, of intellectual virtues such as fair-mindedness, open-mindedness, intellectual carefulness, honesty, patience and charity.

Fourth, throughout its history, the Christian church has shown a high and appropriate regard for the enterprise of education. Many Christian parents have a strong and active concern for the quality of their children's education. Other Christians regard teaching as their vocation, as an important and meaningful way to live out their Christian faith. To the extent that we share such a concern or calling, we must ask: What exactly *is* a good education? What do we want our children or students to derive from their many years in school? Presumably, we want them to acquire a good deal of knowledge. We also want them to cultivate a range of intellectual skills: we want them to learn to read, write and think proficiently. But it is not difficult to see how a person might receive these things from her education without actually having received a fully satisfactory education. Or a person might leave high school or university with a lot of knowledge and intellectual skills but without actually *caring* about learning and knowledge—without a commitment to pursuing these things in her life beyond school.

Sometimes this missing element is referred to in terms of a "love of learning" or a commitment to being a "lifelong learner." But these concepts are rarely unpacked or explained. If they were, the value in question would be identified as that of intellectual virtue. An important part of what we want for the education of our children and students is that they develop a deep and abiding love of knowledge: a love that gives rise to curiosity and attentiveness to the world around them; a desire to continue learning about a broad range of subject matters, and to be tenacious and disciplined in this pursuit; a willingness to question their beliefs and the beliefs of others but also to have the courage of their convictions; and an inclination to treat foreign ideas fairly and respectfully. If this is right, then to the extent that we as Christians are, as we should be, concerned with the enterprise of education, we must also cultivate an interest in and understanding of matters of intellectual character and virtue.

Where does this leave us? We have seen, first, that there is a striking lack of familiarity with matters of intellectual character and virtue at the academic and popular levels and, second, that this is something about which Christians should be especially concerned. Fortunately, the lack of scholarly attention to the intellectual virtues has begun to be remedied in recent years with the advent of "virtue epistemology," which is an approach to epistemology, or the philosophical study of knowledge, that gives a central role to reflection on these traits and their role in a good intellectual life. However, this concern with intellectual virtues has yet to "trickle down" to a nonacademic audience. What is needed, then, is an informed, accessible and engaging account of the intellectual virtues that will help the average reader to understand just what the intellectual virtues *are* and how we might go about *acquiring* them—and, ideally, an account that approaches these issues from a richly and distinctively Christian standpoint.

This need is met perfectly in the present book. Philip Dow has been thinking carefully about the intellectual virtues for years. And he has had extensive experience incorporating a concern with intellectual character and virtue into school curricula and classrooms across the globe. The result is a masterful and deeply insightful treatment of the intellectual virtues, how they are acquired, their role in the intellectual life and their significance from a distinctively Christian standpoint. Dow's writing is accessible, engaging and fun. It is also intellectually astute, historically informed and packed with wonderful illustrations. I have very high hopes for this book. I hope it will begin to open the public's—and especially the church's—imagination in such a way that the notions of intellectual character and virtue will begin to occupy the central role they deserve in our everyday thinking about and assessment of ourselves and the world we inhabit.

Jason Baehr
Loyola Marymount University

INTRODUCTION

Sometimes, when I consider what tremendous
consequences come from little things, . . . I am
tempted to think . . . that there are no little things.

BRUCE BARTON, QUOTED IN *THE SEVEN*
HABITS OF HIGHLY EFFECTIVE PEOPLE

IN 1521, A DEVOUT CATHOLIC PRIEST RISKED HIS LIFE because of his allegiance to the truth. Armed with little more than the strength of his convictions and a habit of courageous thinking, Martin Luther stood before some of the most powerful men in the world and refused to recant his beliefs, stating, "Unless I am convinced by Scripture and plain reason, . . . I cannot and will not recant anything, for to go against conscience is neither right nor safe. Here I stand. I cannot do otherwise. So help me God."[1]

Less than a hundred years later, an impoverished young math teacher, fueled by a desire to understand God's universe, began to carefully investigate claims about the cosmos that contradicted the conclusions of much of the scientific community—not to mention the current religious orthodoxy, common sense and two thousand years of tradition. Johannes Kepler's spiritually inspired willingness to consider the evidence fairly and carefully led him to the conclusion that the earth was not the center of the solar system but, in fact, revolved elliptically around the sun.[2] This breakthrough, and others by the young Lutheran mathematician, provided the foundation for Newton's theory of gravity and a host of additional scientific discoveries and unleashed untold numbers of inventions and advances that have transformed our lives for the better.

Yet another 150 years later a small and sickly British parliamentarian, convinced that God had created all people in his image, helped initiate a campaign to end slavery that would last almost fifty years and put him regularly at odds with some of the wealthiest and most powerful men in the British Empire. Dismissed and ridiculed as a religious enthusiast, William Wilberforce responded by earnestly applying his mind to the issue. He read everything there was to read on slavery, actively sought out former slaves and other firsthand witnesses of the trade, and carefully evaluated the mounting body of circumstantial evidence he had accumulated. So thoroughly did he come to understand the issue that, without the aid of notes, Wilberforce regularly produced before parliament rigorously detailed and carefully reasoned speeches lasting for hours at a time. In an age when oratory was judged by substance as well as style, Wilberforce's arguments against slavery were considered unsurpassed. If the young parliamentarian's strength was an honest and careful mind, his thinking was no less tenacious, for it took twenty years of constant labor before the first real breakthrough occurred and another twenty-six years, just three days prior to his death in 1833, before the practice of slavery was entirely abolished in the British Empire.[3]

Each of these men risked his life, overcame tremendous odds and battled through deep personal disappointments because he believed that pursuing the truth was inseparable from his Christian faith. They all believed their minds were a sacred gift, to be developed and used in the service of their neighbor and to the glory of God. Posterity remembers these men, and we admire them, not because of a single virtuous thought or act but because their passion for the truth had, over time, produced in them a set of admirable thinking habits—habits that led them to the wise insights, breathtaking discoveries and cultural reforms that transformed their lives, the lives of those around them and, ultimately, the course of history itself.

Casting our eyes about our communities today, we might be forgiven for asking where all the Luthers, Keplers and Wilberforces have gone. It is not as though breakthroughs have ceased to occur or that moral reformers have disappeared, but when we honestly evaluate the thinking habits of our culture, the dominant impression we get is not a pleasant one. Whether it is in the slippery words and deeds of our politicians, the ethical vacuum that is our popular media, or the deceptive advertising and marketing strategies employed by our businesses, instead of thinking that is honest, careful, courageous and fair-minded, what we find is rampant dishonesty, carelessness, cowardice and bias.

Of course, we are not shocked by the deceit of our political and cultural leaders, and why should we be? The newspaper headlines are only the natural outcome of the same cancer that we see eating away at our local communities, families and individual lives. It seems that in our communities the allegiance to the truth often appears to end where self-interest or the pursuit of pleasure begins. Recent polls, for instance, indicate that almost two-thirds of American students cheat on exams—a form of intellectual deceit that all too easily spills over into our relationships, as evidenced in other studies that suggest that as many as half of Americans will cheat on their partners.[4] It is easy enough to point an accusing finger at anonymous statistics like these, but when we take a brutally honest look at our own lives, we see the same dynamics at work. We may not cook the books or lie under oath, but our thinking habits reflect the same patterns we condemn in our leaders. The consequences may not seem as dramatic, but the subtle habits of deception that we nurture out of the glare of the public spotlight nevertheless carry consequences that are just as painful.

There are all kinds of reasons for this apparently widespread loss of virtue, but at its core the crisis is rooted in our thinking habits. By that I don't mean that we have somehow become less intelligent, or even that our education system is falling apart. The problem is deeper than that. The crisis is at the very center. It is a crisis of what some are now calling "intellectual character."[5]

What is intellectual character? When we think of character, we usually think of moral character—that is, we think of moral habits that have been repeated so often that they have become inseparable from who we are. Our intellectual character influences our lives just as moral character does, and with at least as much force. The only difference is that intellectual character is concerned not with our actions as much as it is with the thinking habits we are developing as we seek and use knowledge. Put another way, intellectual character is the force of accumulated thinking habits that shape and color every decision we make. Because our minds tend to lead our actions, in a very real sense the quality of our intellectual character even trumps moral character in terms of its power to direct the course of our lives. Take a minute to consider the influence of intellectual character on our decision-making process.

We tend to think of our choices as isolated moments of decision in which we reason through the pros and cons before making the best choice we can based on the information that we have. In reality, most of the choices we make are not the result of conscious and deliberate reasoning. Whether it is a product of the flood of mental distractions and the frenetic busyness of our modern lives or simply exhaustion, we end up making most of our choices on mental autopilot. We don't reason so much as react, and in this haste we are usually forced to rely on the mental ruts our thinking patterns have produced. These mental ruts are our intellectual character. If we have trained our minds in the direction of good thinking habits, our mental autopilots will generally produce good choices, and good choices generally produce good outcomes. If we have not actively sought to develop the character of our minds, then the prognosis is less encouraging. If these little decisions never amounted to much, it wouldn't really matter, but the problem is that in the accumulation of these little choices the trajectory of our lives is set. In other words, the quality of our mental autopilots matters a great deal.

But our intellectual character does not just influence the multitude of small, everyday choices that fly under our mental radar. Whether we were aware of it or not, the big decisions that command our attention in a much more deliberate way are equally shaped by the thinking patterns we have developed over the years. Let's say I am deciding whether to buy my first house. Over the years, if I had not been practicing virtuous thinking habits such as tenacity (a determination to keep after an idea until I have understood it), carefulness (an insistence on ensuring that important details are not missed) or courage (a willingness to ask questions even when it betrays my ignorance and injures my pride), I would walk into the real estate office with none of the information or intellectual tools I would need to make a wise decision. At that moment I could commit myself to thinking as hard as I possibly could, but the intellectual capital just wouldn't be there. In that way, intellectual character is like a bank that we can invest in or withdraw from. Every choice we make to train and improve our minds is another dollar in the bank. Every time we decide to be lazy or flippant in our thinking we are taking another dollar out. When we come to make big decisions in life, we want to find an account overflowing with intellectual capital, not one long overdrawn.[6]

The power of intellectual character to transform every part of our lives should not come as a surprise to Christians. When Paul was urging the believers in Rome toward radical Christian transformation, he said that if they really wanted to be different, if they wanted to stand out as models of Christlikeness, then they needed to start with the renewing of their minds. And why? Because Paul understood that, for good or ill, the habits of our minds trickle down into every part of our lives—from our spiritual lives to our marriages and from our jobs to our recreation. It was because of this that the writer of Proverbs pleaded, "Though it cost all you have, get understanding. Cherish her, and she will exalt you; embrace her, and she will honor you" (Proverbs 4:7-8).

The purpose of this small book is to help explain what intellectual character is, why it is so important and how we can become people of "virtuous intellectual character." To do this we will explore seven of the most important intellectual character traits: courage, tenacity, carefulness, curiosity, fair-mindedness, honesty and humility. After considering the many benefits to our lives that accompany intellectual character, we will wrap things up with some practical suggestions of how we can nurture good thinking habits in our own lives and in the lives of our children and our communities.

The development of intellectual character is one of the most important and life-changing quests anyone can embark on. But as the very heart of Jesus' command is to love God with all our minds, the pursuit of intellectual character is particularly important to Christians. Yet, whether you are already a Christian or someone interested in becoming one, it is my hope that this book will encourage you to take up the challenge of becoming transformed by the renewing of your mind.[7]

courage

carefulness

tenacity

fair-mindedness

curiosity

honesty

humility

THE SEVEN
INTELLECTUAL
VIRTUES

1

Intellectual Courage

---

*A decline in courage may be the most striking feature which
an outside observer notices in the West in our days.*

Alexander Solzhenitsyn,
address at Harvard Class Day
Afternoon Exercises,
June 8, 1978

You know courage when you see it. The fireman who charges
into the flames of a collapsing building to save an infant's life is
courageous. The woman who refuses to recant her beliefs, knowing
that she will be burned at the stake is courageous. But how do you
know this? What makes these acts courageous?

If the fireman who risked his life rescuing the young child
were suicidal and the fact that he saved the infant was accidental,
would his act still be considered courageous? Or if our martyr
died because she had refused to recant her conviction that a pack
of little purple elves was behind global warming, would her act
still be seen as equally heroic? Or finally, if either of our heroes
had only thought about being courageous, or had simply felt
courageous, but had never acted, would we consider either of
them courageous?

My guess is that to each of these questions, most of us would say no. These acts can no longer be considered courageous, at least not in the truly noble sense of the word. So, for something to be courageous, the motivation behind the deed must be good, reasonable and acted upon. The same things can be said about intellectual courage.

Those who are intellectually courageous earnestly want to know the truth, and so they take risks in the pursuit and promotion of truth. They are willing to reconsider their own beliefs, even if this scares them. But once they have done so, and come to a belief about what is true, they are willing to stick to their guns, even if the majority mocks or threatens them.

We now have a good understanding of what intellectual courage is, but why does it matter and what does it look like? Intellectual courage is not necessarily the most important of the virtues, but it is indispensable. As C. S. Lewis said, "You cannot practice any of the other virtues without bringing this one into play. . . . [It is] the form of every virtue at the testing point."[1] Honest thinking, for instance, almost always includes the likelihood of personal sacrifice and usually includes the frightening prospect of direct confrontation. As a result, it can rightfully be said that if we are not courageous thinkers, we are unlikely to be truly honest thinkers.

The same principle holds true for those who want to be fair-minded in their thinking habits. Reflect on the tremendous courage needed to impartially consider arguments that threaten your most fundamental beliefs. What if you decide they are correct? For me that might include questions like, What if there is no Creator God who loves me personally and gives life its only real meaning? What if all of this is, as Freud and others have claimed, simply wish fulfillment? The whole world, as I have understood it, would come crashing down. The very foundation of my life would be betrayed as a sham. Talk about a frightening possibility. But if I want to be a genuinely fair-minded person, there are times when I am required to give a hearing to deeply threatening ideas—and that requires tremendous courage. In this way, intellectual courage can play a critical role in the exercise of all the intellectual virtues.

When Martin Luther was brought before the Holy Roman Emperor and accused of heresy, the choice before him seemed clear. He knew that by recanting he would be offered positions of privilege and prestige in European society. He also knew that if he refused to recant his beliefs, he would almost certainly face relentless persecution and excommunication, if not death. Faced with these options, Luther nevertheless refused to deny his convictions.[2]

I would be surprised if Martin Luther were not besieged by fear as he stood before his accusers. He knew that the threats of the authorities were more than idle words. He had seen the horrible deaths suffered by heretics in Europe. And yet, his commitment to truth trumped his fear and helped to open the floodgates of social, religious and political reforms that today we call the Protestant Reformation. The movement that Luther inspired was not blameless, but the basic pursuit of truth that was at its core unleashed advances that ultimately helped to produce modern democracy and astonishing material and scientific achievements.[3] It is possible that these advances would have happened without the intellectual courage displayed by Luther on that particular day in that particular city, but they wouldn't have happened without someone displaying courageous thinking—for growth and progress require risk, and risk requires courage.

Martin Luther is a dramatic example of intellectual courage leading to growth and progress, but for most of us, growth comes from little acts of bravery in our daily lives. Consider the young student deciding whether to raise her hand in class. If she does raise her hand, she is risking the mockery of her peers, who will either see that she doesn't understand the material or tease her for being overly enthusiastic. Yet, without this small act of courage, her growth is stunted. She begins to fall further and further behind, and a self-fulfilling cycle of fear and ignorance is initiated. Contrast that with the confidence she gains as she grasps the content and can use that knowledge as a base to understand more advanced concepts as they are introduced. So whether it is Martin Luther or a young schoolgirl, the principle is the same. Courageous thinking habits are at the heart of growth and progress. If, as H. L. Mencken is said to have remarked, "the one permanent emotion of the inferior [person] is fear—fear of the unknown, the complex, the inexplicable,"[4] then it is equally true that the one permanent trait of the intellectually virtuous person is courage—courage to challenge frightening ideas and courage to stick to your guns when you become convinced of the truth.

There is just one thing to add. If Martin Luther had chosen to think, and ultimately act, in an intellectually courageous way only once, there is a strong likelihood that we would never have heard of him. He certainly would not have had the sort of influence on the world that he did. We know about Luther and we admire his courageous thinking only because, as a result of thousands of apparently insignificant choices throughout his life, intellectual courage had become a part of who he was.

It has been said that a person's character is forged not in one dramatic moment but in the ledger of his or her daily work. In the same way, if we want to become people of intellectually courageous character, the war will not be dramatically won or lost in a single brave choice but rather quietly through a multitude of apparently insignificant courageous decisions. The elementary student who regularly risks the mockery of her friends by raising her hand to admit she doesn't understand something, the college student willing to publicly challenge his professors, and the boss who risks losing her authority by changing her mind when she sees she has been wrong—these less dramatic, but no less difficult moments are where the battle for character is won or lost. Only when we win these small skirmishes will we form the habits that ultimately morph into intellectually courageous character.

Intellectual Carefulness

It is more from carelessness about truth
than from intentionally lying that
there is so much falsehood in the world.

Samuel Johnson, Dr. Johnson's Table Talk

When John F. Kennedy announced that America would put a man on the moon by the end of the 1960s, most people chalked it up to political grandstanding or arrogance. However, the time, energy and money (vast amounts of money) that soon began pouring into the American space program made the skeptics sit up and take notice. Within months, NASA announced a series of ambitious plans culminating in a manned trip to the moon. A key component of this program was the exploration of the atmosphere of Venus through the use of *Mariner 1*. Using state-of-the-art technology, this craft was expected to reach speeds of up to 25,820 miles per hour on its trip to Venus before unveiling 9,800 solar cells that would power the vessel while its computers investigated the unknown composition of the Venusian atmosphere. It was to be a multimillion-dollar leap forward for NASA and a signal to the Russians that the Americans were gaining the upper hand in the space race. Unfortunately, four minutes after takeoff, *Mariner 1,* America's national pride with its multimillion-dollar price tag, crashed into the Atlantic Ocean. The cause? It appears that a single symbol had been accidentally omitted from the instructions fed into the craft's computer. Not a great day at the office for that particular rocket scientist.[1]

The story of *Mariner 1* is an example of the dramatic consequences that an act of carelessness can have, but it is not necessarily a good illustration of intellectually careless character. In fact, it is reasonable to assume that the tiny error that doomed that spacecraft was an uncharacteristic act of carelessness by an otherwise intellectually careful person. If you are in any doubt of this, imagine NASA as a community of people who were habitually careless in their thinking. The space program that eventually put people on the moon would never have gotten to square one because in this field accuracy and precision are essential to every detail, of every step, of every project. Ironically, *Mariner 1* failed so dramatically precisely because of NASA's culture of intellectual carefulness. It was the space program's consistent meticulousness and self-conscious attention to detail that had allowed it to produce an unmanned spacecraft with the astonishing capacity to travel to Venus. An *act* of intellectual carelessness may have led to the explosion of *Mariner 1,* but it was a *culture* of intellectual carefulness that had made the mind-boggling successes of the U.S. space program possible.

The same principle is at work in our individual lives. As human beings, we are inevitably going to make some careless mistakes in our thinking. Even the most careful thinker is not totally immune from errors resulting from exhaustion or our inability to handle the overabundance of details flooding our busy lives. And yet, if we are able to develop the habit of thinking carefully, the general trajectory of our lives will be fundamentally changed for the better. We might still lose a proverbial satellite from time to time, but without the habit of careful thinking, the chance for success in our lives will continually struggle just to get off the ground.

The example of *Mariner 1* has one more important lesson for us as individual thinkers. Just as in NASA's aspirations to put a person on the moon, our pursuit of the truth in every area of our lives almost always includes the risk of failure. Sometimes the risks are large and call for extraordinary caution, but it is also possible to become so careful and fastidious about getting things perfect that we never risk and therefore never grow. The student whose fear of getting the answer wrong keeps her from answering a test question and the secretary so concerned about misspelling a word that he reads over every memo thirty times are examples of carefulness gone awry. William James said excessive intellectual carefulness "is like a general informing his soldiers that it is better to keep out of battle forever than to risk a single wound."[2] If fear of making a small error petrifies us and keeps us from seeking to know and understand God and his world, carefulness has become a vice—not a virtue.

But that sort of excessive fastidiousness is not intellectual carefulness. Those who are intellectually careful earnestly want to know the truth; thus they are reasonably and consistently careful that they do not overlook important details and habitually avoid hasty conclusions based on limited evidence. They are patient and diligent in their pursuit of knowledge. Aristotle wisely noted that the intellectually careful person looks "for precision in each class of things just so far as the nature of the subject admits."[3] The intellectually careful and prudent doctor, for instance, will not give the same amount of attention to mowing her lawn as she would to diagnosing her patient because the stakes and circumstances do not warrant equal time. But that does not mean that she ceases to be careful when she mows her lawn or prunes her rose bushes. In fact, her decision to use just the right plant food, or to set her lawnmower blade at just the right height, is directly linked to her ability to carefully and successfully diagnose the ailments of her patients. By consistently choosing to think carefully about how to nurture her garden, the doctor is developing intellectual habits that show up in every area of her life—something for which her patients are extremely grateful.

The problem for most of us is that we see intellectual carefulness as something we can turn on and off at will instead of something that always needs to be turned on but used in proportion to the demands of the circumstances. Because we do not actively develop a consistent pattern of conscientiousness, we may think carefully in isolated moments but do not become intellectually careful people. As a result, when a situation demands careful thinking, we find it difficult to override the hasty and careless thinking patterns that have become the mind's default operating system. The fact that we fail to be adequately careful in our thinking is usually not the fault of our intentions but simply the result of our being out of practice.

Unfortunately, the weeds of intellectual carelessness and hastiness seem to grow effortlessly and bring with them consequences that can be sobering. The case of *Mariner 1* is a dramatic instance of carelessness, but examples of intellectual carelessness do not have to be spectacular to be significant. In the academic world, neglecting to use quotation marks and not citing a source can mean expulsion for students and the loss of a job or a severely damaged reputation for professors. Plagiarism is often intentional, but quite regularly it is simply the result of intellectual carelessness. The Pulitzer Prize–winning author David McCullough's reputation was damaged, and the credibility of his otherwise outstanding biography of John Adams was undermined, because he attributed to Thomas Jefferson a key quotation that Jefferson never spoke.[4] McCullough's apparently careless error quite reasonably raises the question of whether other equally significant errors have been included in his works. There is every reason to believe McCullough's error was an unintentional anomaly in a generally stellar career, but if other errors are found, the credibility of his once highly respected works could very well collapse like a house of cards. The reason? Intentional deception and intellectual carelessness both produce lies, and people don't trust liars.

Another slightly different form of intellectual carelessness that seems to be rampant in our culture is intellectual hastiness. In his famous address to Harvard University, Alexander Solzhenitsyn argued that the media's desperate attempt to meet society's insatiable demand for news pushes it toward "guesswork, rumors and suppositions to fill in the voids, and none of them will ever be rectified, they will stay on in the readers' memory." The result, Solzhenitsyn argued, is countless "hasty, immature, superficial and misleading judgments."[5] The consequences of the media's intellectual hastiness seem to be everywhere. In March of 2006 three members of the Duke University lacrosse team were accused of rape by a North Carolina woman. Almost as soon as the accusations were made newspapers and magazines across the country were writing sordid accounts, filled with unsubstantiated innuendo and complete with strident moral judgments. The *Los Angeles Times* said the young men were examples of a college sport's culture that was "out of control, fueled with pampered athletes with a sense of entitlement," and *Rolling Stone* magazine ran its story under the headline "Sex and Scandal at Duke." Well before any evidence had been examined, the players had been declared guilty in the court of public opinion. The problem was that, while the Duke athletes had put themselves into a morally compromising situation, the accusations had been false.[6]

In the Duke case, reputations were ruined. But consider a real jury made up of people who have developed the habit of either jumping to conclusions or failing to closely examine the evidence that is available. More to the point, consider the nineteen-year-old kid mistakenly condemned to a life in prison because the jury made up their minds after the prosecutor's opening statement. Intellectual hastiness can have serious consequences.

Of course, few of us *consciously* rush to judgments in situations of such gravity. Yet in the so-called little things we are often guilty of habitually hasty thinking. How often, for instance, do we uncritically accept casual office gossip or leap to hasty judgments about others based on innuendo or flimsy circumstantial evidence? If you are anything like me, the answer is far too often. Not only does this form of intellectual hastiness lead to reckless judgments against colleagues—creating a lens through which we then begin to unfairly interpret all other information we hear about them—but it inevitably influences our actions toward those people. Even if we never explicitly pass on our unsubstantiated impressions to others (which we almost always do), our intellectual hastiness has poisoned a relationship and probably affected the way that person is treated in our community. If you are still tempted to think that intellectual character has little to do with practical Christian living, try loving your neighbor as yourself while practicing intellectual hastiness. It can't be done.

A lack of confidence is another natural attribute of the habitually careless or hasty thinker. Consider the following example. Nigel and Jess are on their honeymoon and decide that they would like to try parachuting. From an early age Nigel has been taught to dot his "i's" and cross his "t's." His love of truth was also enough to push him to take reasonable intellectual risks, but when he goes to pack his chute, Nigel's habitual intellectual carefulness serves him well. He listens closely to the instructions and follows them faithfully. Then he goes back and double-checks his work. Nigel's brilliant and carefree bride, on the other hand, has always gotten by on her natural smarts and charisma. So when it comes to packing her parachute, Jess wings it. On the ground both are equally relaxed, but standing on the edge of the plane's door, ten thousand feet up, their experiences are worlds apart. Nigel is excited about the jump, knowing that his chute is sound and set to function perfectly; Jess is rightly paralyzed with fear.

The consequences of her carelessness are obviously potentially tragic for Jess, but for the sake of pleasantness let's say that she gets lucky and her chute still functions properly. Even though they both made it to the ground safely, the thinking habits they had developed prior to the jump still had an important influence on their experience. Rooted in the confidence gained from his habit of careful thinking, Nigel's experience was one of unabashed exhilaration while Jess's intellectual carelessness rightly produced intense and paralyzing fear. Paying close attention to evidence and taking care that we don't hastily pass over important information will not only produce a higher rate of success in every area of our lives, but it will also necessarily create the peace of mind and confidence needed to tackle life's opportunities and obstacles.

When we choose not to develop habits of careful thinking, the consequences to our personal, professional and spiritual lives can be as dramatic as they are harmful. By contrast, the fruits of habitually careful thinking are deceptively mundane. Spaceships get to their destinations and back safely, offices effectively accomplish their goals because employees trust each other's work, our relationships blossom, and our gardens bloom.

Like all the intellectual virtues, intellectual carefulness is not something that we can turn on and off at will. Instead, it is something that we develop over time if we are willing to work at it. By consistently and actively choosing to examine evidence closely, and by refusing to jump to hasty conclusions even in life's apparently unimportant moments, our minds, and then our lives, will slowly be transformed.

3

INTELLECTUAL TENACITY

---

*The only people who achieve much are those who want
knowledge so badly they seek it while conditions are
still unfavorable. Favorable conditions never come.*

C. S. LEWIS, "LEARNING IN WAR TIME"

WHEN I THINK OF TENACITY, the picture that always comes to mind
is that of a tiny terrier that has latched onto some poor victim's
trouser leg and won't let go—ever. That sort of dogged determination is one of the most important character traits a person can
possess. In both our actions and our thinking habits, tenacity is
often the difference between success and failure, fulfillment and
frustration. Let me illustrate this truth with a metaphorical example from my own home.

Recently my four-month-old daughter was sitting in her "magic
chair" carrying on an animated discussion with the purple and
pink elephant dangling in front of her. As some catchy music
played in the background, I got the idea that it would be fun to try
to teach her how to clap. So I sat down on the floor next to her and
began to sing and clap along to the tune. As she watched curiously,
I held her hands and continued to sing, bringing her hands to-

gether as I did. In the weeks just prior to this, my obviously brilliant daughter had become more aware of her hands, sucking on her fist regularly and even reaching to touch her inanimate friends. Still, clapping was asking a lot of a four-month-old, and I knew it.

Not surprisingly, the first time I tried this she smiled but little else. The next day I decided to try again. After helping her clap initially, I set her hands down and continued to clap on my own. Then, after a couple of moments had passed, an extremely serious look crossed her face, and, almost imperceptibly at first, both hands began to move upward and toward each other. The whole process took at least a couple of minutes and consumed every ounce of concentration and effort she had to offer, but in the end—for as little as a second—two hands clumsily connected before dropping in exhaustion by her side.

What I had just witnessed was a remarkable example of tenacity and a wonderful window into the initial stages of character formation. As I type, my fingers fly across the keys, gliding from one key to another with effortless efficiency. That dexterity is something I take for granted. It is natural to me—second nature. But Emma showed me that what has become natural to me is the result of a lifetime of training my muscles to move with speed and accuracy—a process that began with excruciatingly difficult first movements and grew only through long and difficult practice.

There are very few things that I value in myself or others that did not come about through this painful process of stretching and striving. And yet, when it comes to our individual thinking habits, and those of our society, tenacity has lately fallen on hard times. Neil Postman and the late Allan Bloom pin some of the blame on TV, while William Bennett and others have argued that sustained prosperity has made us soft. Whatever the cause, it is hard to avoid the conclusion that we have a tough time sticking with something when the going gets tough.[1] The impressive number of hours the average American continues to work each week only masks the deeper and more disturbing trend we see in our consumer culture toward a something-for-nothing mentality that champions the easy quick fix over a hard-earned cure. This culture of cutting corners can survive for a time, but its cosmetic commodities cannot ultimately replace real achievement, and real achievement always requires tenacity. Nowhere does this truth have more significant consequences than in our thinking habits.

A few of my friends from high school have gone on to become successful artists. They followed their interests and abilities and, as a result, have found a vocation in which they feel fulfilled. And yet, while they are doing what they love, all of them have experienced frustrating periods when they were utterly incapable of taking the vision that was in their heads and putting it onto the canvas. Sometimes they simply needed to spend time experimenting with colors and techniques, but there have been other times when no amount of experimenting would help. No progress could be made until they had mastered the new technique or artistic skill that was required to get the result they were after. So for days, weeks or even months, they needed to stop creating and do the hard and painstaking work of learning that new skill. It was not fun, they did not love it, and at different points in their lives, they would all say that they felt like giving up. During those moments, their ability and natural love of art were not enough.

For every artist who achieves the ability to produce work of genuine beauty and value, there are hundreds who fall by the wayside. The difference between these people and my friends is neither talent nor artistic passion. In fact, it is safe to assume that there are failed artists out there with more ability and enthusiasm than my friends have. The difference is tenacity.

The inventor Thomas Edison is credited with remarking that genius is "one percent inspiration and ninety-nine percent perspiration."[2] There is no question that Edison was a brilliant man doing what he loved, yet he recognized that these things were not enough. Edison's insight rings true in every area of life and nowhere more so than in the life of the mind. Just like the artists I have mentioned, Edison knew that real achievement and authentic success require thinking habits rooted in tenacity.

Tenacious thinking is also needed in order to grow beyond our current limitations. Like many artists, my friends do not gravitate toward the hard sciences and even tend to shy away from the so-called social sciences, such as history. They aren't naturally gifted in these areas, and they certainly don't have a passion for them. And yet, without battling through the frustrating process of understanding physics, biology and history, the scope and depth of their art would forever be limited. For example, an understanding of light is central to art, but this understanding cannot be completely achieved without doing some hard work in physics. In addition, great art is usually informed by a thorough understanding of human psychology and history, but that also requires long hours of studying well outside the boundaries of many artists' natural inclinations. The point is simply this—to produce great art the artists are often required to think in areas outside of their natural aptitudes and interests. At least initially, it is usually not much fun. And yet, the knowledge that waits on the other side of the struggle can be life changing. Without tenacious thinking habits, the promise that awaits each of us will forever remain out of reach.

But is tenacity always a good thing? Like all the intellectual virtues, tenacious thinking can be pointless or even harmful if its aim is not noble. What makes tenacious intellectual character praiseworthy is its ultimate aim of seeking goodness and truth. A person who spends an entire life trying to count the number of ants in the backyard cannot be considered virtuous—at least not in the same sense as a person tenaciously pursuing a cure for cancer. In addition, to be praiseworthy, tenacious thinking must also be balanced against the other important components of our lives. For instance, the man whose noble pursuit of a cleaner-burning fuel leads him to ignore his wife and children for months on end cannot be admired morally, even if he is a shining example of intellectual character.

These qualifications aside, it is hard to overstate both the goodness and the importance of tenacious thinking habits in our lives. One final anecdote will serve to highlight several additional benefits of developing intellectually tenacious character. Good friends Suzie and Jackie are both reading *War and Peace* for a class in European literature. About ten pages in, Suzie decides she is bored with the book and makes the choice to stop reading it. As a consequence of her decision, she does get to spend more time watching reruns of *Friends,* but it also means that she misses a chance to understand a key period in Russian history and a chance to grow personally by wrestling with the moral and political issues raised by this classic. For some of us, this tradeoff doesn't sound too bad. However, although Suzie's natural smarts might allow her to slide by with a passing grade, she hasn't forced herself to learn how to think well. As a result, she will come to the next novel lacking the analytical skills needed to succeed in understanding it fully—not to mention entering her college European history class with almost no foundation for understanding modern European politics and culture. When she travels to Europe (because Rachel on *Friends* said in one show Europe was cool), all she sees are old buildings and the occasional McDonald's—the one thing she does understand. Suzie's ignorant and untrained eyes simply have not developed the capacity to see any of the fascinating cultural richness that surrounds her. When Suzie shut the novel and flipped on *Friends,* she didn't, in one step, condemn herself to a dull, flat and shallow life. But by choosing the natural and easy path, she began digging the rut of intellectual laziness that will inevitably lead her there.

Jackie also finds the first pages boring. She too is faced with a subtle fork in the road of her life. But, instead of turning on the TV, she decides to press on. Things don't instantaneously and miraculously improve for Jackie. In fact, it is not until page three hundred, after fighting to stay interested, that she begins to understand and appreciate the novel. But when she does finally finish the novel, Jackie's whole world has changed. Because she stuck with it, she has wrestled with some deep moral and spiritual questions and come to a rich understanding of them that inspires her to act differently. In addition, she approaches the next novel she reads with honed analytical abilities and a multilayered foundation of knowledge that allow her to approach the novel at a deeper and more fulfilling level. When she reads the *New York Times,* she understands the current dilemmas in Russia far better than Suzie does, not because she is smarter but because she understands the historical foundations of the culture. The chances are good that, when the grades come out, Jackie's mark will reflect her work, but even if her tenacity does not reap immediate rewards, she has begun to develop the thinking habits and knowledge base that will profoundly and positively alter the course of her life.

There is one last important outcome of Jackie's choice to battle through the initial drudgery of *War and Peace*—the sense of accomplishment that comes at the end. I realize that this sentiment sounds a lot like the sort of thing your parents said to you when you were begging them to let you quit your violin or piano lessons as a kid, but we all know it is true. There is something deeply satisfying about completing a task, especially when that task included significant obstacles or hardships. Handing in that science project, finally figuring out the solution to that algebraic equation or putting that last period on a challenging but well-written business proposal can all be tremendously satisfying—in large part because they were difficult. As Thomas Paine famously wrote at the lowest point of the American Revolution, "What we obtain too cheap, we esteem too lightly. . . . Heaven knows how to put a proper price upon its goods."[3] Of the many rewards that come from intellectual tenacity, few are more life giving than the sense of achievement in the face of tremendous odds.

4

INTELLECTUAL FAIR-MINDEDNESS

In this kind of learned contest the real victory
lies in being vanquished. Even the weakest, consequently,
ought . . . to seek them out . . . for the one who is bested
receives from his conqueror, not an injury but a benefit;
he returns to his house richer than he left.

GIOVANNI PICO DELLA MIRANDOLA,
ORATION ON THE DIGNITY OF MAN

SOMETIMES WHEN TRYING TO GET a clear picture of what something is, it is helpful to begin by saying what that something is not.
This is certainly the case with intellectual fair-mindedness. When
we think of fair-mindedness, we usually think of openness. Today,
however, openness is often understood in relativistic terms—the
belief that all ideas should be equally valued and accepted. A commitment to relativistic openness has influenced our society to such
a degree that the late Allan Bloom observed, "Almost every student
entering the university believes, or says he believes, that truth is
relative."[1] This situation is exacerbated because fair-mindedness
and relativistic openness can look and sound like the same creature
while remaining fundamentally opposed to each other. If we want

to nurture openness (fair-mindedness), we need to confront the threat that relativistic openness is to our intellectual life. There are a host of reasons why the relativistic sort of openness is dangerous. For starters, in the area of education, relativism ultimately leads to the demise of learning. A playful example from a first-grade math class will help illustrate this.

Imagine a young and enthusiastic elementary school teacher beginning to teach addition to her first-grade class: "Add one apple to another apple and you get . . . two apples; two oranges plus two oranges equals four oranges . . ." Suddenly a precocious whipper-snapper interrupts, "But my family believes that two plus two equals five!" As a few students snicker and others applaud their friend's valiant stand on behalf of intellectual freedom, the teacher has at least two options. She could respond by thanking him for his opinion but assuring the class that two plus two does, in fact, equal four. Alternatively, in the pursuit of openness, she could also respond, "Okay, Jimmy, for you, two plus two can equal five." Jimmy's self-esteem is intact—for the moment—but his teacher's application of relativistic openness has begun to destroy the foundation upon which all of Jimmy's additional mathematical learning must take place. Assuming he remains true to himself, Jimmy's false mathematical principles will mean that higher math will be impossible for him to master and that when he works the register at the local 7-Eleven, somebody is going to lose a lot of money. Relativistic openness has hurt Jimmy, not to mention the customers at 7-Eleven and everyone else impacted by his teacher's desire to promote "openness." At best, the relativistic brand of openness hinders learning; at worst, it makes learning impossible.

But isn't relativistic openness only applied to matters of opinion? And, if so, doesn't that make the math example a bit of a straw man? As ridiculous as it may seem to us, most facts that we base our lives on were at some point also mere opinions. The fact that the world is a sphere, or that it revolves around the sun, were opinions at one time, much like a belief in a flat earth. Yet, a belief that the truth about reality could be understood encouraged people to pursue answers. That pursuit led to a greater under- standing of the world and its place in our solar system, which, in turn, led to countless additional findings that have transformed our daily lives. Relativistic openness puts an end to that quest by assuming that many things are not objectively knowable. And be- cause they are not knowable, we are better off accepting all an- swers as equally valid than embarking on a potentially acrimo- nious search for the right one. The principle found in Jimmy's story is not just applicable to the hard sciences; it holds true wherever learning is being pursued. When we stop believing in truth, the virtue of fair-mindedness morphs into meaninglessness, and the end of education is not far away. As G. K. Chesterton said about relativistic openness, "There is a thought that stops thought."[2]

Relativistic openness also makes us gullible. The moment that we come to believe that all ideas are equally true is the same moment when it no longer makes sense to question the validity of ideas. It doesn't take a rocket scientist to see that when we stop critically evaluating ideas, the consequences, sooner or later, will be disastrous. In the early 1500s the radical reformer Thomas Müntzer was facing a crisis in his peasant war against the authority of the German princes. His band of several thousand peasants was getting ready to confront a powerful force of well-equipped and hardened soldiers. Knowing the peasants were afraid, the charis- matic Müntzer promised them that anyone who followed him into battle would survive unharmed. Instead of asking whether his words were true, over six thousand men enthusiastically ran headlong toward their deaths. Only a handful escaped alive.[3] It is unlikely that these peasants were relativists, but they remain a good example of the gullibility that relativistic openness naturally creates. They had stopped critically analyzing the truth claims of their leader, and the result was catastrophic.

Relativistic openness also undermines progress for the simple reason that progress assumes a goal. We only know we are making progress when we are getting closer to that goal. Take away the goal of truth and any talk of advancing becomes meaningless. All our attempts at moral, scientific or spiritual improvement simply become nonsense unless we believe that there are targets we are shooting for. This is the great dilemma of our time. Everywhere you go, in every arena of life, everyone is striving, but when we are asked what we are striving for, the best most of us can offer is a blank stare. Relativistic openness has not been able to dull our need for purpose, but it has managed to make that quest a confused and jumbled mess. As C. S. Lewis said, "Such is the tragic-comedy of our situation—we continue to clamor for those very qualities we are rendering impossible. . . . We castrate and bid the geldings be fruitful."[4]

It should be clear by now what fair-mindedness is not. It is not relativistic openness. What might remain unclear is what fair-mindedness is and what it might look like in practice. Let's start with a basic definition. Those who are fair-minded earnestly want to know the truth and thus are willing to listen in an even-handed way to differing opinions, even if they already have strong views on the subject. In addition, they attempt to view the issue from the perspective of their opponents, believing that they do not always have the most complete or accurate vantage point on a given issue. The secret of intellectually fair-minded persons is that they have chosen to put the truth above allegiance to their ego or cherished opinions. Without that basic commitment to truth, authentic fair-mindedness is not possible.

The fifteenth-century thinker Giovanni Pico della Mirandola is a good example of the spirit of intellectual fair-mindedness. In

1486, della Mirandola was a young man whose life was being transformed by the pursuit of learning that the Renaissance had inspired in his city. In his enthusiasm, della Mirandola offended
some important people and several times was asked to answer for
some of his unorthodox opinions. Even in open-minded Renaissance Italy, public criticism by political and religious leaders was
comparable to a social and intellectual death sentence. Yet, instead
of shying away from public criticism, della Mirandola wrote a
short book in which he embraced the public examination of his
ideas as the best way to get to the truth.[5] In one passage, he sums
up his attitude saying, "In this kind of learned contest the real
victory lies in being vanquished. Even the weakest, consequently,
ought . . . to seek them out . . . for the one who is bested receives
from his conqueror, not an injury but a benefit; he returns to his
house richer than he left."[6] In other words, della Mirandola was
saying, why should I fear criticism of my views? What could be
better than finding flaws in my thinking and, therefore, growing
further in my understanding of the truth? Della Mirandola's love
of the truth overcame his natural inclination to shelter his opinions.
This is the core of fair-mindedness.

Becoming a fair-minded person is no small thing. For a whole
host of reasons, the determination to hold on to our current
opinions is deeply ingrained in our nature. For proof of this, just
think back to the silly arguments of your childhood, or if that is
too long ago, think back to the petty arguments you have already
had this week. One's ego naturally and zealously guards its territory, making the choice to fairly consider other perspectives extremely difficult.

Putting the pursuit of truth above the satisfaction of our egos is
a considerable challenge, but when we do it, the rewards are plen-
tiful. The most obvious and far-reaching benefit that naturally
comes to the intellectually fair-minded person is more knowledge.

Della Mirandola argued that when listening fairly results in the conclusion that your original opinion was wrong, it is a cause for celebration! That's right. Not only does it mean that your understanding of the world is better than it had been, but in accepting this new knowledge, you also inherit the many rewards that this greater knowledge will bring.

Among the many other benefits that come to the intellectually fair-minded person, two stand out but in very different ways. One is relatively abstract and the other is ridiculously practical, but both are equally life changing. Let's begin with the abstract benefit. The fair-minded person is much more likely to escape from a prison of false assumptions. A historical anecdote will illustrate the point.

As we have already seen, in the seventeenth century a European stargazer by the name of Johannes Kepler became fascinated by the blanket of stars that covered the night sky over his town and committed himself to a greater understanding of the heavens. Thanks to Aristotle, for two thousand years the Western world had assumed that the universe revolved around the earth. The Catholic church was convinced that it had interpreted key passages in the Bible in line with the Aristotelian view, essentially making Aristotle's views the views of all good Christians. Not only had church doctrine been built around this theory, but almost all scientific inquiry had been rooted in the same set of assumptions. So foundational was this perspective that instead of questioning their assumptions, those people who had noticed inconsistencies between the Aristotelian view and the way the universe actually behaved simply created ever more extravagant explanations for how these inconsistencies were in harmony with the commonly held view.

What separated Kepler from his predecessors, beyond the accumulating evidence undermining the accepted view, was his willingness to look at the evidence in a genuinely fair-minded way. It

is unlikely that Kepler was any more intelligent than the many
smart people who had considered the heavens before him. He was,
however, willing to consider other possible explanations for the
evidence, and the results transformed our understanding of the
universe. Kepler's discovery that the planets in the solar system
revolved around the sun ultimately led to Newton's groundbreaking understanding of gravity and a host of other innovations
that form the foundation of science today.[7]

Alfred Whitehead made the observation that some "assumptions appear so obvious that people do not know what they are
assuming because no other way of putting things has ever occurred to them."[8] In that way our assumptions often act as an intellectual prison keeping us from truth. Like Kepler, the fair-minded
person is someone whose habit of considering questions from
other perspectives has become so deeply ingrained that he or she
is rarely caught in the prison of unexamined assumptions.

Now let's consider the ridiculously practical benefit of fair-
mindedness. Genuinely fair-minded people will always make and
keep friends more easily than people whose thinking habits are
close-minded or biased. Among the many reasons for this, perhaps
the most important is the inherent link between fair-mindedness
and listening. Because they are committed to discovering the truth,
fair-minded people listen—they really listen. For persons of fair-
minded character, listening well is not simply a skill used to con-
vince others that they care; they really care about the truth and as
a result they listen. Very few things give people a greater sense of
their own value and worth as individuals than being truly heard.
Being given this kind of attention tells us that our views have significance, and, therefore, so do we. And nothing attracts us to another person more than a belief that that person values us.

I'll grant you that, beyond being fair-minded, there are other
reasons people may grow into being good listeners. A person who

is romantically attached to another person, for instance, is likely to display the characteristics of a good listener (although many a spouse may beg to differ with me on this point). But even when we include other possible reasons for people to be good listeners, there remain some important differences between the fair-minded person and other people who display good listening skills. For starters, romantically involved listeners—and most other categories of listeners—are motivated by external forces that come and go. In this case, they are influenced by the ebb and flow of their emotional life. The waxing and waning of the romantic listener undermines the message of inherent worth and value that the consistency of the fair-minded listener creates.

People can also display good listening skills when they are genuinely impressed by others. As a high school student I sat in awe of my US government teacher. In his class I listened with rapt attention, asking follow-up questions and generally soaking in everything he had to say. I was an excellent learner, and he responded to that by pouring time and energy into my growth. The problem was that these admirable qualities did not follow me as I walked into other classrooms. The quality of my listening was not a matter of intellectual character but the product of external forces (in this case my admiration for one teacher). Because I was less enamored with my other teachers, I missed out on a tremendous amount of personal and intellectual growth they were offering me. My personal biases cut me off from a wellspring of knowledge, not to mention negatively affecting my relationships with my other teachers. In contrast, the fair-minded person consistently makes the choice to reject preconceived prejudices and takes the thoughts and opinions of all people seriously. Making the choice to listen fairly on a consistent basis has become so deeply ingrained in fair-minded people that it is their default setting. It is what comes naturally for them. By consistently treating everyone with equal worth, the intellectually fair-minded person communicates respect and dignity to many who are overlooked based on shallow prejudice.

As we have seen, relativistic openness and fair-mindedness often look deceptively similar in practice, but they are fundamentally different perspectives that bear dramatically different fruits. Relativistic openness rejects a belief in transcendent truth and therefore undermines the learning process and the concept of progress while leading us toward lives of shallow gullibility. Fair-mindedness, on the other hand, is rooted in the idea that truth not only exists but that it can be found when, by consistently seeking the truth over the satisfaction of our egos, we slowly become fair-minded people. This is the openness that invigorates learning, builds a solid foundation upon which to live, and leads us toward lives of wisdom, richness and depth.

5

INTELLECTUAL CURIOSITY

Now the Berean Jews were of more noble character
than those in Thessalonica, for they received the message
with great eagerness and examined the Scriptures
every day to see if what Paul said was true.

ACTS 17:11

SHORTLY AFTER THE END OF WORLD WAR II, a young British doctor joined the staff of the Vellore Hospital in India. Dr. Paul Wilson Brand had grown up in India as the child of missionaries, but after many years of education and training in England, his return to India was a shock to his system. The scale of suffering he saw, particularly among the many Indians stricken by Hansen's disease (leprosy), almost overwhelmed the young physician. Inspired by his evangelical conviction that those suffering were children of God, Brand began searching for answers to the medical mystery that was Hansen's disease.

Over a number of years, Brand discovered that the root cause of many leprosy-related deformities was injuries resulting from the inability of the leper to feel pain. This breakthrough led him to pioneer a variety of successful treatments for those suffering from

Hansen's disease around the world, revolutionizing the way Hansen's disease was viewed and transforming the lives of hundreds of thousands of its victims, especially among the poorest populations of the world's developing nations.[1] Brand passed away in 2003, but the legacy of his faith-inspired intellectual curiosity will be positively changing lives for many years to come.

Dr. Brand's life had all the hallmarks of intellectual curiosity. His earnest desire to know the truth inspired him to habitually ask the all-important why questions. In addition, this desire to understand what makes it all work—at the foundational level—forced him to go beyond the shallow or simplistic answers that most of us accept but that produce no growth. Instead, his curiosity pushed him into ever more challenging (and fulfilling) intellectual ventures. Finally, his quest for knowledge was not simply a necessary evil (the means of getting a good job and buying a house) but a morally driven and lifelong pursuit of truth. His life also demonstrates that, while it may not be the most important of the intellectual character traits, intellectual curiosity is the most foundational. Without the desire to know more, growth in every area of our lives is virtually impossible.

If curiosity is the most foundational of all the intellectual virtues, it is also the one that raises the most eyebrows. Didn't curiosity kill the cat? Isn't unbridled curiosity dangerous? The children's book character Curious George, for instance, is constantly getting himself into trouble because of his ever-inquisitive mind. More seriously, curiosity is regularly held responsible for all sorts of addictions. The following anecdote from the life of Isaac Newton highlights both the dangers and the merits of intellectual curiosity.

As a young man, Isaac Newton had become so alive to the wonder of creation that his thirst for truth occasionally led him to risk his own safety. In an attempt to understand how people perceive light and color, the young Newton went so far as to wedge a flat stick between his skull and the back of his eye. By pressing the stick against the backside of his eye, Newton wrote, "There appeared several white, darke and colored circles which were plainest when I continued to rub my eye with ye point of ye bodkin."[2]

It's enough to make an optometrist squirm, and it certainly isn't something you should try at home, but it does illustrate both the rewards and the potential pitfalls of intellectual curiosity. Without it we will never grow in our understanding of anything; yet, unbridled curiosity has the capability of doing real and lasting harm. Our world is a far richer place because Newton was curious, but that would not have been the case had he blinded himself in the pursuit of truth.

If curiosity is not always virtuous, how can we tell the difference between its good and bad varieties? For starters, the curiosity that we should want to develop is motivated by noble aims. That doesn't mean that asking apparently random questions is not good. In fact, creative questions can often lead to the most unexpected and useful insights. That said, Dr. Brand's desire to understand the causes of leprosy in order to help end the suffering of thousands is an example of intellectual curiosity that is clearly praiseworthy because its aim is noble. By contrast, the sort of morally suspect and self-indulgent curiosity that motivates a young teen to dabble in pornography is not.

The good sort of curiosity is also balanced against the potential pitfalls that any given line of inquiry may take. This is especially the case in areas where general knowledge has already established the negative effects of a certain piece of knowledge. We do not need to leap from the Empire State Building, for instance, in order to prove that falling hundreds of feet can be fatal. In the same way, the teen who justifies experimenting with drugs based on a desire to understand the effects of drugs for herself is exhibiting a lack of common sense, not intellectual curiosity.

While the latter examples are fairly obvious, there are other cases that may appear to be legitimate examples of the good sort of curiosity but are nevertheless more accurately regarded as intellectually reckless. The recovering gambling addict who wants to help other addicts by investigating the inner workings of the Las Vegas casino industry may be motivated by a good aim, but the risks to his own moral character probably outweigh the potential rewards. As my former university administrator used to say, if you're on a diet, you probably shouldn't take a job at Baskin-Robbins.³ If we were always the angelic pursuers of altruistic truths that we would like to be, intellectual curiosity would always be good. As it is, the reality of human moral frailty means that a reasonable amount of critical self-awareness and caution should always accompany intellectual curiosity.

Those qualifications aside, intellectual curiosity remains one of the most important and foundational of the intellectual virtues. Unless we are in the habit of asking the why questions, we will remain in neutral, never growing and never experiencing the richness that comes from a well-examined life. Consider the following classroom dialogue between George, a likeable but goofy high school nerd who seems incapable of stopping himself from asking questions in class, and his teacher, Mr. Jones.

Mr. Jones: "The Pilgrims came to Plymouth in 1620."

George: "Why did they come? And why then?"

Mr. Jones: "Because they wanted to practice their faith freely."

George: "Why couldn't they do that in Europe?"

Mr. Jones: "Because in Europe there was a close relationship between the established church and a political system which felt threatened by those who believed differently."

George: "Why did the European establishment feel threatened?

. . . And how did this affect the way the Pilgrims viewed the relationship between religion and politics? . . . And how does that
affect America today?"

And on and on and on it goes. As annoying as George's questions may be for his peers, and perhaps even his teachers, with
each why question, George is peeling back another layer of life's
richness and seeing new connections that allow him to think and
live a more meaningful, effective and abundant life. We don't need
to be in a classroom to ask good questions and reap the results. In
fact, the same enriching process is probably even more powerful
when it is applied to our day-to-day lives.

Unlike many of the other intellectual virtues that must be con-
scientiously learned and practiced, we seem to enter the world already wired for curiosity. As our parents have probably told us, we
used to drive them batty with all our questions when we were
young children. Unfortunately, whether it was the mockery of our
peers in school, a fear of betraying our ignorance or the assumption
that we know as much as we need to know, somewhere along the
way, most of us have gotten out of the habit of asking the why
questions. To the degree that this has happened, we have also
ceased to grow intellectually. If this stunted growth were only
found in areas of our lives apparently far removed from practical
living—let's say, the use of color by Cézanne or the intricacies of
higher mathematics—then we might be forgiven for concluding
that our lack of intellectual curiosity was harmless. The chances
are, however, that a lack of curiosity in one area of our lives is only
a symptom of a more pervasive mental atrophy.

The good news is that, because we all have at least the remnants
of the curious habits of our childhood, intellectually curious character is easier to develop than the other virtues. For many of us,
reactivating the powerful force of intellectual curiosity may be as

simple as taking ten minutes each day to investigate a topic we have been interested in but haven't taken the time to explore. Or, it might mean picking some random reality and asking why it is the way it is. Why, for instance, does Starbucks often choose to put two coffee shops on opposite corners of the same intersection? Why, for a few years, did teenage boys in America choose to wear their jeans around their knees instead of their waists? What might explain recent research findings that North Dakotans are the most outgoing people in America?[4] Whatever the question, don't stop with the first layer of answers. They rarely produce any growth or any useful insights. Keep digging. I guarantee that you will be surprised at the useful and interesting insights that this sort of exploration can produce.

Intellectual Honesty

You cannot play with the animal in you
without becoming wholly animal [or] play with
falsehood without forfeiting your right to truth.

Dag Hammarskjöld, *Markings*

Unlike the other intellectual character traits, intellectual honesty is not primarily about the process of *getting* knowledge but rather about how we choose to *use* or *present* the knowledge we already have. In that sense, intellectual honesty is the link between the rest of our thinking and our actions. Whether presenting a groundbreaking theory or making an argument in casual conversation, the aim of intellectually honest people is to communicate what they know with integrity. Because their main objective is to help others get at the truth, they are consistently careful not to use information taken out of context, to distort the truth by describing it with loaded language or to otherwise mislead through the manipulation of statistics or any other type of supporting evidence. In addition, intellectually honest people do not take credit for evidence or ideas that are not their own, and so are careful to cite the work of others whenever it is used. The intellectually honest person's motto is summed up in the old court oath, to tell "the truth, the whole truth and nothing but the truth." Of all the intellectual virtues, honesty is perhaps the most practical and the most admired. Unfortunately it is also probably the least practiced.

In 2003 the *New York Times* took the first of a series of major blows to its reputation as a trustworthy news source. In an unprecedented front-page article, the editors admitted that up to six hundred of their articles, written by Jayson Blair, had been either partly plagiarized or simply made up. It later became evident that in his zeal to rise up the chain of reporters, Blair had consistently put his career and his opinions above the pursuit of the truth. As a result, millions of people had not only ingested fabrications but had almost certainly had their opinions of the events around them shaped by those lies.[1]

At the peak of the 2004 U.S. presidential campaign, CBS News ran a story claiming that the current president and Republican candidate had refused to obey the orders of his superiors while in the National Guard and had used influential friends to intentionally embellish his service record. Because the story cast serious doubt on the candidate's trustworthiness and pointed to a fundamentally self-centered cowardice in George W. Bush's character, it would have made the headlines in any election year. But this year it was an even bigger deal. The 2004 election had essentially turned into a referendum on Bush's leadership in the controversial Iraq war, and anything that could significantly undermine the president's credentials as a wartime leader would likely hand the election to his Democratic challenger.

There was just one problem. The story appeared to have been based on forged documents. Even worse, despite the fact that they knew the story could change American history, Dan Rather and the editors at CBS News not only didn't properly check out their source; they went ahead with the story even after significant questions were raised about the documents' veracity.[2]

In 2005 one of the world's leading stem-cell scientists, South Korean Dr. Hwang Woo Suk, was forced to admit that much of the research that had propelled him to national and international stardom had been doctored to achieve the results he wanted. The revelation sent shock waves through the scientific community, which had already begun to pour large sums of money and time into building on Hwang's breakthroughs.[3]

For Jayson Blair, the motive appears to have been his ambition to rise to the top. For CBS, it could have been either zeal for an exclusive scoop, or perhaps even desire to influence an important election. And for Dr. Hwang, it might have been any number of things—academic respect, international fame or wealth. Whatever the variety of motives, all three stories have one important thing in common—in each case the actors wanted something else more than they wanted the truth.

Alexander Solzhenitsyn in his address to Harvard University remarked that, "Western society [is now] based . . . on the letter of the law. . . . People . . . have acquired considerable skill in using, interpreting and manipulating law. . . . If one is right from a legal point of view, nothing more is required, nobody may mention that one could still not be entirely right. . . : It would sound simply absurd."[4] When we take the time to consider Solzhenitsyn's words, it is hard to think of a stronger condemnation of our culture. In essence he is saying that while the appearance of truth and justice is still important to us, we have little use for the real thing—unless it can be manipulated to help us get what we want.

We only need to open up our daily newspaper to see that Solzhenitsyn was right. Whether it is the billions of dollars lost in the accounting scandals of companies like Enron or the blatant twisting of the truth by our political leaders or our advertisers, dishonest thinking habits are rampant at the very highest levels of

American society. It shouldn't surprise us that these high-profile examples are nothing more than the continuation of patterns we are nurturing on our playing fields and in our classrooms. The children's soccer coach who tells his players to put winning above integrity and the parent who places the importance of grades above real learning are both guilty of encouraging the sort of thinking patterns that lead to intellectually dishonest character. The evidence that American children are learning these lessons all too well is on display in classrooms across the county.

Cheating is hardly unique to America, and to claim that it is a new phenomenon is just this side of ridiculous. And yet, the pervasive nature of academic dishonesty in America today is a disturbing indication that intellectual honesty has fallen on very hard times. A recent survey of eighteen thousand high school students by Rutgers University Professor Donald McCabe confirmed what other studies have been suggesting for years—that approximately two-thirds of American students cheat on exams. (And that is only the number of students who admitted to cheating.)[5]

It is unsettling that students are cheating en masse, but more significant still is the habitual nature of cheating and the long-term consequences this habit has on society and the students themselves. Studies over the last forty years have shown that those who cheat in high school continue to cheat in college and beyond. In other words, acts of intellectual dishonesty are not simply isolated events but can become a fundamental part of who we are; and when this happens, the consequences to our lives, and to the society we live in, are devastating.

The most obvious, but in some ways the least destructive, consequence of intellectual dishonesty is that we can—and usually do—get caught. In 1979 Dr. Bob Harris was rapidly reaching the peak of his dream career. For a number of years he had been a TV weatherman for a well-known New York station and been hired as a consultant by both the *New York Times* and the commissioner of baseball, Bowie Kuhn. That year, an anonymous letter prompted an investigation into his credentials. Not only had Harris never received the Ph.D. from Columbia that he claimed, but he had not even finished his bachelor's degree. The consequences of his deception came with devastating speed. He was immediately fired by both his TV station and the *New York Times*. And while he did manage to keep his position with Commissioner Kuhn, Harris admitted that his deception had played a role in his divorce. Said Harris, "I took a short cut that turned out to be the long way around, and one day the bill came due. I will be sorry as long as I am alive."[6] Bob Harris not only lost his job and the prestige of association with the *New York Times* but would spend the rest of his life trying to overcome the stain on his character.

As Bob Harris's divorce illustrates, acts of deception are rarely quarantined to one area of our lives. During his days as a rancher, one of Teddy Roosevelt's cattlemen caught an unbranded renegade steer on his neighbor's land. Although the honor code stipulated that the steer should have been his neighbor's, the ranch hand began to apply Roosevelt's brand to the steer. As soon as Roosevelt realized what was happening, the ranch hand was packing his bags. A furious Roosevelt was understood to have said, "Now you go straight back to the ranch and get whatever is owing to you. . . . If you will steal for me then you will steal from me."[7] The moral: our relationships are built on trust, and when we are found to be deceptive in one area of our lives, we sabotage the potential for gaining and keeping the trust of others. And when that happens, our chances of developing meaningful and happy relationships are poisoned.

But in a very real sense the Bob Harrises of the world are the lucky ones. In a number of ways, the consequences of intellectual dishonesty can be far worse for those of us who are never found out. To begin with, when we persist in using or manipulating knowledge in dishonest ways, we begin a battle with our conscience that, unless our conscience wins, will have one of two equally negative outcomes. The first possible outcome is a life weighed down by the debilitating load of guilt. We have all experienced the heaviness of unconfessed guilt. By contrast, while intellectual honesty is often the more difficult road, it is always the one characterized by greater freedom.

There is a second outcome that may be even worse than living with guilt, for it leads to the death of our conscience and endangers our souls. Dallas Willard has argued that instead of our ethics guiding our behavior, our behavior often guides our ethics. In other words, we often do what we want and then create a moral code that suits our actions.[8] While it is often difficult to see this process unfold in our own lives, most of us have witnessed this process of moral deterioration in friends and acquaintances.

Let me illustrate with a fictional anecdote. Jimmy and Jenny are high school sweethearts, regular members of their church youth group, and believe strongly that sex outside of marriage is wrong. In a moment of weakness, Jimmy and Jenny decide to break their own rules. The feeling of guilt is almost immediate, but instead of confessing their failing (something that would bring considerable public shame), they successfully hide their action. Unwilling to reveal their secret, the only remaining way to escape from the ever-increasing weight of guilt is to redefine their idea of what is right and wrong. If sex outside of marriage is, in fact, not sinful, then there is nothing to feel guilty about. And so, the evolution of their ethics begins. The same phenomenon is at work in our thinking habits, and the result is a corrupted intellectual conscience that no longer values the truth, if it can still distinguish the truth from falsehood at all.

Granted, the total inability to discern the truth from a lie can only result from a lifetime of habitual dishonesty, but to the degree that we choose to manipulate or dishonestly use knowledge, we risk losing our taste for truth. As former Secretary General of the United Nations Dag Hammarskjöld wisely noted, "You cannot play with the animal in you without becoming wholly animal [or] play with falsehood without forfeiting your right to truth."⁹

So far we have examined the impact of dishonest thinking habits on the individual and his personal relationships, but the influence of intellectual dishonesty on the larger society is considerable. Of course the most obvious influence of intellectual dishonesty on a society is found in the cumulative effects of so-called personal intellectual ethics. For it is these choices that either build up or tear down trust among colleagues, friends and family; and it is these relationships that are the foundation of a culture. As a result, any culture in which intellectual dishonesty reigns at the individual level will reap the consequences on a societal scale as well.

However, there are other ways that intellectual dishonesty can impact the larger society. For starters, whenever we choose to manipulate information, we help to construct a false foundation of knowledge that others will unwittingly build upon. The more significant the claim, the more devastating the potential effects of intellectual dishonesty will be. A well-known example of this effect of intellectual dishonesty is that of the Piltdown Man.

In 1911 Charles Dawson, a highly regarded amateur geologist, discovered fossilized human remains in a gravel pit in Sussex, England. When the remains were presented to the British Museum a year later, they seemed to fit (almost exactly) the predicted development of humans that evolutionary theorists had hypothesized. Almost in unison, the scientific community and the mass media trumpeted the discovery as one of the greatest in the study of human origins, and Piltdown Man become a centerpiece of evolutionary orthodoxy. For the next forty years, scientists devoted entire careers to explaining the finding's significance and developing its implications.

In 1953 a skeptical South African anatomist asked the British Museum for permission to carry out further tests on Piltdown Man. The tests conclusively proved that Piltdown Man was not a 500,000-year-old human ancestor but the combination of a 1,000-year-old male skull and the jaw of a modern female ape that had been chemically and manually altered to give it the appearance of significant age. Piltdown Man was a hoax.[10]

The example of Piltdown Man is important for a number of reasons. As we have already seen, through their act of intellectual dishonesty, the creators of the hoax were directly responsible for the tremendous amounts of time and energy that hundreds of outstanding minds wasted in an attempt to build on Dawson's fallacious discovery—not to mention the millions of dollars lost. The example of Piltdown Man can also shed light on another phenomenon linked to the vice of intellectual dishonesty—that of rationalization.

From the overwhelming and uncritical acceptance of the Piltdown discovery, it appears that the scientific community and the popular media were already predisposed to believe what Dawson and his friends were offering, and this made it difficult for them to critically assess the legitimacy of Dawson's claims. Further, while no other evidence was found that corroborated the Piltdown discovery, for forty years scientists continued to awkwardly force new findings into the false premises established by the hoax. Dallas Willard calls this "use of reasoning to make sure that one comes out at the right place"—rationalization.[11] To the degree that we put any goal above our allegiance to truth, we are all tempted to use our reasoning ability in this fundamentally dishonest way. Whether we are six-day creationists, theistic evolutionists, liberal democrats or right-wing republicans, the need to be aware of how our belief system and our ulterior motives affect our pursuit of the truth is a lesson we must take seriously.

In this chapter we have spent a long time looking at the vice of intellectual dishonesty and the harm that it does to individuals, relationships and society at large. But there is, of course, another side to this equation—the tremendous rewards that result from consistently acting in an intellectually honest way. Among other things, honest thinking habits inevitably build the trust between people that is at the core of healthy personal relationships, healthy communities and healthy cultures. Although it is increasingly rare, when we see it, honest thinking habits in our political leadership also go a long way toward restoring the public confidence in the political system that is essential to enthusiastic and widespread participation in the political process. Finally, honest thinking at all levels of society is what produces the necessary true foundation upon which knowledge and progress can advance.

From the multitude of examples of intellectual dishonesty we come across daily, it is clear that choosing to consistently think with integrity is not easy. In the short term, holding yourself and others to intellectual honesty can undermine your own beliefs, threaten friendships or compel you to confront deception in the workplace. That said, every time we choose to present hard truths honestly to friends, shareholders or the electorate, we are building momentum toward honest thinking habits that can positively transform our lives and the lives of those around us. If every subtle intellectually dishonest act chips away at the health of our relationships, poisons the pursuit of knowledge and undermines the trust essential to our political and economic freedoms, then every intellectually honest act is an equally powerful step in the opposite direction.

INTELLECTUAL HUMILITY

If a man would make his world large,
he must be always making himself small.

G. K. CHESTERTON, *ORTHODOXY*

IF IT IS NOT THE MOST IMPORTANT of the intellectual virtues (and it very well might be), intellectual humility is almost certainly the most misunderstood. So what does it mean to be humble in the way we think? Some of us have come to believe that it means thinking that everyone is smarter than we are and knows more than we do. As C. S. Lewis has observed, for many, humility means "pretty women trying to believe they are ugly and clever men trying to think they are fools."[1] But that can't be it. Not only is this sort of reasoning dishonest, but when applied to our thinking habits, it can cripple our ability to learn and grow. As G. K. Chesterton warned, adopting this definition of humility can put us on the road "to producing a race of men too mentally modest to believe in the multiplication table."[2]

Unlike the false humility that Lewis and Chesterton describe so well, authentic humility is simply an attempt to see ourselves as we really are. Applied to our thinking, this means an uncompromisingly honest appraisal of the capacities and limitations of our minds against the standard of an all-knowing, infinitely intelligent and always true God. This reality check can be simultaneously heartening and sobering.

According to the Bible, we are created in God's image. This means that we are born as rational and creative beings with the capacity to find and apply truth. This should be a source of immense encouragement to us. However, Scripture and reality both teach that our minds are also finite and tainted by the effects of sin, giving us good reason to approach both our own reasoning and the knowledge of others with a healthy degree of skepticism. In his book *The Captive Mind*, Czesław Miłosz recounts an old proverb to the effect that "when someone is honestly 55% right, that's very good and there's no use wrangling. And if someone is 60% right, that's wonderful, it's great luck, and let him thank God. But what's to be said about 75% right? Wise people say this is suspicious. Well, and what about 100% right? Whoever says he's 100% right is a fanatic, a thug, and the worst kind of rascal."[3]

In other words, to the extent that we are rooted in reality, we will be intellectually humble; and this humility will extend not only to our own intellectual capacity but also to how we assess human reasoning generally. That sounds simple enough. The problem is that seeing ourselves as we really are is easier said than done. The tendency of modern culture to ignore evil and our own unwillingness to face the depravity in our own thinking make us all too eager to place excessive confidence in reason. While it may make us feel good in the short term, this distorted self-image fundamentally undermines intellectual humility.

Further harm is done to the cause of humility by our tendency to judge the quality and capacity of our minds not by the standard of an all-knowing Creator of an infinitely complex universe but in competition with the knowledge and intelligence of our neighbor.

The problem with this is that when we consistently judge the quality and capacity of our thinking against theirs, we will always end up with either a deceptively high or low view of ourselves, and this makes it difficult to see our thinking habits and capacities as they really are. When this happens, the foundation upon which authentic intellectual humility is built cannot be laid.

Intellectual humility is notoriously elusive, but when it does become a habit, the rewards can be life changing. Because intellectually humble people value truth over their egos' need to be right, they are freed up to admit the limits of their own knowledge. This freedom naturally produces a teachable spirit and the habit of humble inquiry that are at the heart of sustained personal growth. This does not mean that humble people are necessarily wrong or that, upon reflection, they will change their minds. It only means that they are submissive to the truth and are, therefore, capable of expanding their understanding of the world in a way that arrogant people are incapable of doing. The following story from the life of Abraham Lincoln is a remarkable example of intellectual humility under difficult circumstances.

At the height of the American Civil War, President Abraham Lincoln was doing everything in his power to preserve the unity of his crumbling country. As both the nation's elected president and as one of the most intelligent men of his generation, Lincoln had every right to expect deferential respect from his subordinates. And yet, as the war waged, he found himself being criticized and ridiculed by friends and foes alike. One man Lincoln was supposed to count as a friend was his secretary of war, Edwin Stanton. However, both publicly and privately Stanton had made no secret of his disrespect for Lincoln. Even though Lincoln was aware of Stanton's insubordination, Lincoln kept his secretary of war, believing that Stanton's sharp mind and independent perspective would be a valuable balance to his own.

At one of the war's most critical points Lincoln sent a direct order to Stanton. Not only did Stanton refuse to carry it out, but he again publicly mocked Lincoln, calling him a fool. Instead of reacting out of anger or spite, Lincoln is said to have replied, "If Stanton said I was a . . . fool then I must be one. For he is nearly always right, and generally says what he means. I will step over and see him."[4] Lincoln was no wimp. He had demonstrated many times over that he was more than willing to buck the opinions of others if he believed they were wrong. Still, as the story goes, the two men had a meeting in which Lincoln listened carefully to his subordinate, concluded that Stanton was right and withdrew his order. Lincoln ignored the demands of pride in order to pursue the wisest course. Ultimately, this intellectual humility helped save his crumbling nation and ensured that he would go down as one of the greatest statesmen in the nation's history.

In addition to the growth of knowledge and insight that comes from intellectual humility, the person whose thinking is consistently humble will also be rewarded with a world far larger and richer than the one inhabited by the intellectually proud person. Consider this analogy from history. Over centuries of self-consumed privilege, some of the French aristocracy had developed an almost complete ignorance of the plight of the common person. As a result, when the riots over bread prices that sparked the French Revolution had finally become so serious that the aristocracy was forced to take notice, legend has it that the French king's wife, Marie Antoinette, famously remarked, "Well, let them eat cake." Generally interpreted as a reflection of the French aristocracy's disdain for the peasants, the statement was really a reflection of the horrific level of ignorance that existed among the aristocracy. This ignorance was not a result of a lack of education or intelligence. It was simply the natural consequence of the aristocracy's long-held arrogant disregard for anything outside of their tiny and isolated world. In contrast to the French nobility, intellectually humble people understand that the larger our egos are the less space there is left in our minds for anything or anyone else.[5]

If the intellectually humble person is rewarded with a bigger world, he or she is also freed up to enjoy that world in a way that the intellectually proud person cannot. As C. S. Lewis pointed out, "Pride is essentially competitive in nature. [It] gets no pleasure out of having something, only out of having more than the next man."[6] In that way, pride not only keeps us from enjoying the insights and achievements of others, but it builds up walls of suspicion and resentment between us and the very people whose thinking can enrich our lives. While we find this dynamic at work in every area of our lives, the academic world is particularly plagued by the poison of intellectual pride. For instance, when a lab produces a major breakthrough in the fight against some disease, the reaction of the competing labs is usually not joy that this breakthrough will save thousands of lives but jealousy that the breakthrough was not theirs. In fact, it is likely that even the joy felt by the successful scientists doesn't come primarily from the goodness of their breakthrough but from the fact that the breakthrough was theirs.

Intellectual humility is not like this. Because intellectually humble people love truth more than their own egos, they are freed to enjoy the goodness of knowledge and insight regardless of where, when or in whom it is found. In *The Screwtape Letters*, C. S. Lewis uses a fictional dialogue between two demons to describe the type of joy and freedom that can come from intellectual humility. Writing to the junior demon Wormwood, Screwtape says, "The enemy [God] wants to bring the man to a state of mind in which he could build the best cathedral in the world, and know it to be the best, and rejoice in the fact, without being any more (or less) or otherwise glad at having done it than he would be if it had been done by another."[7] This pure and unadulterated joy can only be experienced when we value truth above ourselves.

Finally, because intellectually humble people see themselves not as owners but as good stewards of the truth, they are almost always more generous with knowledge than the intellectually proud person would be. This should not surprise us. Every day we see the same dynamic at work in our material lives. Unlike those who see their material possessions as "on loan" from God, people who view their material possessions as personal property are much more likely to lock up that hard-earned property and to guard it jealously. In the same way, those who treat truth as a commodity to be bought and sold are unlikely to simply give it away without getting something in return. Like Gollum's self-destructive obsession with the ring in Tolkien's novels, when we see knowledge as something to possess, not only do we miss out on the fulfillment of seeing that knowledge positively influence the lives of those around us, but we miss out on the rich personal growth that results from participation in a free give and take of truth.

Because it goes against both the currents of our culture and the pride that is so deeply rooted in all of us, intellectual humility is probably the most difficult of the virtues to develop. Yet once we begin to build up a pattern of humble thinking, the rewards will be profoundly life enhancing. Beyond the unadulterated joy we will experience as our world grows in depth and richness, we will almost certainly find other intellectual character traits such as fair-mindedness and honesty naturally tagging along. That's the way humility works. It is a facilitating virtue. It invites everyone to be a part of the party.

courage

carefulness

tenacity

THE FRUITS OF INTELLECTUAL CHARACTER

fair-mindedness

*But seek first his kingdom and his righteousness,
and all these things will be given to you as well.*

MATTHEW 6:33

curiosity

honesty

I first watched the Academy Award–winning film *Chariots of Fire* as a boy with my family. I couldn't have been more than eleven or twelve, but two scenes from the story have stuck with me ever since. In the first scene Harold Abrams, one of the greatest runners in British history, had just won the 100-meter dash at the 1924 Paris Olympics. After four years of single-minded self-discipline and sacrifice, his victory should have been a moment of tremendous fulfillment and exhilarating joy; yet as Abrams and his coach sat quietly in a Paris bar that night, there was a palpable sense of emptiness. Why? Near the end of the scene Abrams's coach gives us a clue. "You know who you won for today?" said Mr. Mussabini. "Us—you and Sam Mussabini."

By contrast, for Eric Liddell the Olympics were not about the pursuit of respect, personal success, wealth or fame. He ran because he loved it, and his love of running was rooted in his belief that by running he was honoring the God who had given him his athletic gifts. "When I run," said Liddell to his sister, "I feel his pleasure." That Liddell was not running for himself became clear in the film when he refused to run in the 100-meter heats because they fell on a Sunday. For what some may have seen as a religious technicality, Liddell was willing to set aside four years of sweat and sacrifice and his dream of running in the Olympics. However, when he was unexpectedly given the chance to run in the 400-meter dash—and miraculously won—the joy and satisfaction seen in Liddell and his family and friends was absolutely infectious.

In a couple of important ways the stories of Abrams and Liddell are virtually identical. Most importantly, both Abrams and Liddell climbed to the pinnacle of their field by winning an Olympic gold medal. They also spent countless hours in training and made deep personal sacrifices to achieve their Olympic dreams. And yet, while they both accomplished their goal, the taste of that achievement in their mouths was radically different. In the end, what mattered was their motivation.

The same principle applies to our pursuit of intellectual character. If we want to enjoy its fruits, our aim must be "the truth, the whole truth, and nothing but the truth." If, on the other hand, we are seeking intellectual character primarily for the attractive by-products we think will come along with it, our efforts will be frustrated from day one. Not only are we unlikely to grow in intellectual character, but whatever fruit we do take hold of is unlikely to have a satisfying taste. As C. S. Lewis put it, "If you look for truth, you may find comfort in the end; if you look for comfort you will not get either comfort or truth."[1] That is the trick. The benefits cannot become our aim.

I only mention this because, as we are about to see, the benefits that come from developing good intellectual character are so many, and so transformative, that there is a real risk of confusing the fruits of intellectual character with the thing itself. That does not mean that we should scorn the good fruit that comes from good thinking habits. Not at all. The benefits of intellectually virtuous character are gifts that God wants us to experience. They are part of our reward, a small taste of heaven, to be received with gratefulness and enjoyed with thanksgiving. In fact, as long as we remain focused on the truth, the promise of enjoying the byproducts of the process can act to spur us on. So what are these good byproducts that come from developing virtuous intellectual character?

The benefits that come to the intellectually virtuous person can be broken down into three categories: We come to know more. We become better thinkers. And we become better people.

THE BENEFITS OF KNOWING
MORE ABOUT MORE

*The eyes only see what the mind
is prepared to comprehend.*

ROBERTSON DAVIES,
IN *WORDSWORTH DICTIONARY
OF QUOTATIONS*

SOME THINGS ARE SO OBVIOUS that they need to be said. One of these things is that intellectual character invariably produces an increase in knowledge, and this increased knowledge, when used morally, almost always produces positive change in our lives. Contrary to folk wisdom, ignorance is usually not blissful. Generally, it produces the very opposite of bliss. Just ask the frightened hiker lost in some remote mountain blizzard who never paid attention to his Boy Scout instruction; or ask the new employee who never did her math homework, frantically trying to figure out the correct change for customers; or, worse yet, ask the frustrated and annoyed patrons waiting in the ever-increasing line as this new employee bumbles one purchase after another.

In contrast, the knowledge that naturally comes from intellectual character does not just decrease our suffering, and the suffering of those around us; it can also substantially increase our enjoyment of the world. As the saying goes, "The eye sees what the mind knows." In other words, our experience of the world around us will only be as rich and textured as the knowledge we have about that world.

To illustrate this principle I used to show my students a poster of Masaccio's *Holy Trinity* and ask them what they thought of it. From my otherwise sharp students, I would get responses like, "It's nice," or "What's the deal with the skeleton at the bottom?" Then, after explaining in some detail both the religious and political events that influenced the painting, and its groundbreaking significance (it was one of the first paintings ever to use "scientific" one-point perspective, which creates the illusion of depth), I would again ask my students what they thought of it.[1] More often than not, the little knowledge they had gained not only made their estimation of the painting soar, but it provoked a tidal wave of new, and excellent, questions. Their increased knowledge had given them new life-enhancing eyes.

The growing knowledge base that naturally results from virtuous intellectual character is also increasingly likely to produce novel insights and creative solutions to problems. For instance, the story that Newton's theory of gravity was simply the product of watching an apple fall from a tree only makes sense when we take into account Newton's already considerable understanding of the laws of physics. Newton was certainly not the first person in the history of the world to observe a falling apple, but he was the first to take that experience and build from it the groundbreaking law of universal gravitation. The falling apple produced the sensational insight it did only because it was analyzed by Newton within the framework of his already vast prior knowledge of the world.[2]

The increase in knowledge we gain as a byproduct of developing intellectual character also makes us more interesting people. While no one likes the arrogant walking encyclopedia whose sole purpose seems to be demonstrating his superior knowledge, there are few things more enjoyable than talking to people who simply love learning. They ask us great questions, listen intently to our answers and then often produce the most unexpected and fascinating connections between what we have just told them and their own prior knowledge. In short, knowledgeable and intellectually virtuous people are almost always interesting people. And in the instances where they are not, they are undoubtedly more interesting than they would have otherwise been.

A person's influence also usually increases in step with the increasing knowledge being accumulated by that person. Among the most memorable American advertisements from the 1970s and 1980s were those that promoted the investment company E. F. Hutton. The scenes were varied, but the plot was always the same. One person would casually mention to another that "my broker is E. F. Hutton, and he says . . . ," at which point everyone on the busy street or in the loud party would suddenly stop and lean toward the speaker in an attempt to listen. Regardless of whether E. F. Hutton deserved that level of respect, the commercials illustrated the influence that comes with an increase in credible knowledge. And this principle certainly doesn't end with Wall Street. Whether you are in a faculty meeting at the local high school, a church Bible study or a meeting of the president's National Security Council, the most respect is given to the people who know the most and who have a track record of providing trustworthy counsel.

We have only begun to scratch the surface in terms of the many benefits that come through the growth of knowledge that naturally results when we grow in intellectual character. Even so, our initial list is impressive. Among other benefits, an increase in knowledge leads to a life that is both less painful (at least as in terms of avoiding the unnecessary pain resulting from ignorance or poor choices) and more rich and satisfying. In addition, the person possessing the depth and breadth of knowledge typical of the intellectually virtuous person is also more likely to be insightful, interesting and influential. Not bad, but the good news is only just beginning.

9

THE BENEFITS
OF BETTER THINKING

---

*The lazy boy in the class is the one
who works hardest in the end.*

C. S. LEWIS, *MERE CHRISTIANITY*

AS WE HAVE JUST SEEN, INTELLECTUAL CHARACTER invariably increases the depth and breadth of our knowledge, and this improving knowledge base can positively transform our lives in a number of important ways. Just as significant are the positive changes that virtuous intellectual character produces in the *way* we think—that is, in our thinking processes and skills. This chapter will look exclusively at the benefits that intellectual character brings to the thinking process itself.

It may seem self-evident that any consistent pursuit of knowledge will produce an improvement in our thinking, but this is not necessarily the case. There are many forms of "learning" that, while producing a form of knowledge, do not positively alter the way we think. Indeed, pursuing knowledge in dishonorable ways can actually undermine the development of good thinking, producing a disastrous ripple effect that touches every part of our lives.

In many parts of the world the educational systems encourage the acquisition of knowledge through rote learning. Students in these schools learn primarily by memorizing large quantities of information and are then judged by exams that seek little beyond a regurgitation of the facts. As a result, while these students often accumulate impressive amounts of knowledge, the thinking habits they develop seriously restrict their capacity to apply their knowledge in useful and fulfilling ways, not to mention hampering the ability of these students to acquire and evaluate any new information that they may confront in the real world.

But the educational system is not the main problem. For most of us, regardless of the system we have grown up within, the real threat to our growth as thinkers resides in our motivation and our will. We want knowledge but only if it comes quickly and easily. Even more dangerous than a faulty system of learning, this virtually universal something-for-nothing mentality fundamentally undermines the growth of quality thinking skills and processes.

Consider the student whose first instinct is to go to the back of the math book for the answers whenever he meets even the slightest of mental challenges. Or to bring us closer to the real world, consider the nurse who, instead of keeping up with the latest advances, relies on the knowledge of other nurses whenever confronted with an unfamiliar medical challenge. In a sense, both of these people get the information they need for the moment. However, beyond the important fact that they don't really understand the knowledge that they supposedly possess (and therefore cannot ever build on that knowledge), by short-circuiting the learning process, they are undermining the growth of the thinking process itself—a reality that has consequences well beyond affecting their ability to do sums, or even to care for the sick. In addition, in their efforts to avoid hard work they are ultimately giving themselves more work and crippling the development of skills (such as critical thinking, fact-checking and problem solving) that would have eventually yielded a steady stream of benefits affecting both themselves and their neighbors.

In contrast, because intellectually virtuous people are motivated primarily by a desire for the truth, they are willing to put in the hard work needed to get to the truth. They self-consciously evaluate the facts that they are committing to memory. They apply this knowledge to real problems. And they seek to understand that knowledge within their ever-expanding appreciation of the world around them. As a result, their desire for the truth not only produces a greater quantity and quality of information; it positively transforms their thinking process and hones their thinking skills. Because clear, efficient and insightful thinking has become second nature for them, in the long run their hard work has made everything easier. Let me briefly illustrate this point with an analogy from the world of sport.

I happen to be a big soccer fan. From as early as I can remember, I have watched and played "the beautiful game." Of all the extraordinary players I have seen in my lifetime, the greatest was a Frenchman named Zinedine Zidane. The things that Zidane could do with a soccer ball, often while running flat out and with defenders tugging at his shirt, were simply unbelievable. I have seen him deftly redirect a fifty-yard goal kick to the feet of a sprinting teammate with the back of his heel. I have seen him curl a shot over a wall of opponents, past the outstretched hands of a diving goalie and into the top corner of the goal from thirty yards out. And I have seen him spin 360 degrees around defenders, while running at top speed, with the ball glued to his feet. And yet what astonished me most about Zidane was the air of effortlessness with which he accomplished all these things.

The apparent ease of his on-the-field artistry might lead the ignorant observer to conclude that Zidane was simply a phenome-

nally talented individual. However, Zidane, his teammates and all
those who watched him grow up know better. The son of poor
immigrants from Algeria, Zidane had become convinced at an
early age that the game he loved was his only chance to help his
family out of poverty. As a result, Zidane dedicated his youth to
soccer—running for miles through the empty streets of predawn
Marseille, juggling the ball for hours in his family's flat, and seeking
out any and all opportunities to test his growing soccer skills.
While certainly a natural talent, Zidane accomplished what he did
through years of sacrifice and dedication. Functioning at top speed
and often at the point of physical exhaustion, Zidane was forced to
rely not on his talents but on the trained instincts, muscle memory
and accumulated knowledge of the game that he had developed
over years of effort. Simply put, the secret to Zidane was practice.[1]

The same is true when it comes to our ability to think well. The
key to unlocking the potential of our minds is not to be found
primarily in our IQ, memory-improving gimmicks or the cost of
our education. The secret to better thinking is wrapped up in the
hard mental work that naturally results from an earnest pursuit of
the truth. To see how this works in practice, let's look at how the
practice of just one of the intellectual virtues (carefulness) can
help produce important and life-altering thinking skills.

From the moment you consciously start practicing careful
thinking, you step onto the path of wise decision making. For instance, you might begin checking out the extravagant claims of
advertisers and making sure your accounts are accurate before
making significant purchases. Before voting, you might seek out
the records of politicians to see if their deeds match their words.
Or you might make sure you have strong evidence before making
hasty judgments about others based on casual office gossip. Each
of these individual decisions to think carefully is likely to produce
obvious, immediate and important benefits.

However, if you continue to practice carefulness, over time your thinking slowly becomes *habitually* careful, and this is where the most critical consequences are seen. For starters, thinking well becomes easier. Unlike those who have to spend an extraordinary amount of time and energy every time they decide that they need to think carefully, habitually careful thinkers have developed thinking skills and patterns of thought that allow them to accurately process knowledge with speed and relative ease. Like Zidane's apparently effortless ability to pass with precision in nearly impossible circumstances, thinking accurately and precisely has simply become part of the careful thinker.

As one intellectual character trait becomes deeply ingrained, it is also likely that evidence of other positive characteristics will soon begin to appear. We have already seen evidence of this principle in our soccer illustration, where the development of one set of physical habits in Zidane (his ability to control the soccer ball) naturally had a positive knock-on effect by improving his ability to pass and shoot as well. The same dynamic is at work in our thinking. For example, careful thinking habits usually lead to correct information, which, in turn, generally produces an increase in confidence. This carefulness-inspired confidence is an essential element in developing the courage necessary to ask questions and to take risks in the pursuit of truth. Intellectual carefulness, therefore, begets intellectual courage. In the same way, intellectual carefulness encourages the growth of both intellectual humility (as our carefulness uncovers our own tendency to make important errors in reasoning) and intellectual fair-mindedness (because it is hard to be fair-minded without carefully assessing the opposing argument). This mutually encouraging domino effect is active in the relationship among all the intellectual virtues. If you begin developing one, the chances are that others will also come along for the ride.

In addition, in the same way that Zidane's long hours of practice and continual efforts to test himself produced outstanding soccer skills, the practice of virtuous intellectual character is responsible for the development of a number of important *thinking skills,* such as problem solving and critical thinking. The following adaptation of an old folktale effectively illustrates how at least three intellectual character traits (carefulness, curiosity and tenacity) can interact to produce these valuable skills and alter the course of our lives in positive and practical ways.

Many years ago, two cousins grew up close friends in a Hawaiian seaside village. They played together, did chores together and, when they were old enough, went to school together. In fact, the only thing that they did not do together was their homework. Both boys found school challenging, but the first boy made a choice early on to apply himself to his studies. He worked hard to understand his teacher, asked questions when he didn't understand and studied after school. The second boy, while also wanting to succeed, chose the easy road, spending his free time surfing, taking shortcuts in his homework and cramming for tests.

In their teens the two boys were sent to different schools and didn't see each other again until they both began working for the local chief—the first boy as the chief's adviser and the second as an oarsman on the chief's yacht. Within a short time, the chief took his annual trip along the coast, visiting his people and listening to their needs. Whatever thrill the oarsman might have had in seeing his friend again quickly began to slip away as, for hour after hot hour, he struggled at the oars while his cousin ate papaya and mangoes with the chief in the cool of the yacht's canopy. One night the oarsman grumbled aloud to his friends, "It makes me sick. After all, we are blood relatives. What gives him the right to relax in the breeze while we suffer at the oars?"

Late that night, after everyone had been asleep some time, the oarsman was awakened by the chief. "A sound coming from the shore is keeping me awake," said the chief. "Would you go and find out what it is?" In no time the oarsman had gone ashore and returned with a report. "It is just a bunch of puppies, sir," said the oarsmen. "Oh? How many puppies?" asked the chief. Of course the oarsman wasn't in the habit of noting important details, and so he returned again to land. Coming back once more, the now breathless oarsman informed the chief that there were seven puppies and triumphantly turned toward his bed. But the chief was not finished. "And how many males and females were there?" he prodded, prompting yet another trip back into the night. "Three males and four females," panted the oarsman after returning. "Thank you," said the chief. "Now come with me."

The chief took the oarsman up to the front of the boat where his advisers were sleeping and woke up the oarsman's cousin. "There is a noise coming from the shore," said the chief. "Could you go and find out what it is?" Just as the oarsman had done, the adviser disappeared into the night and returned quickly to report. "Sir, the noise you have heard is from a litter of new puppies." "And how many puppies were there?" asked the chief. "Seven," replied the adviser. "How many males and females?" continued the chief. "Three males and four females," responded the adviser. "Is there anything else I should know?" prodded the chief. "Yes, sir. The puppies, which are a rare breed of bulldog, were born to the local farmer's prized pet. The farmer apologizes for the disturbance and would be pleased if you would select one of the puppies as a gift."

The chief thanked his adviser, allowed him to return to his bed, and turned to the oarsman. "I heard you complaining today. You may think that it isn't fair, but I had to send you to the village three times tonight; and even then I lacked some important information. I only had to send your cousin once. That is why he is my adviser, and you are an oarsman."[2]

In contrast to the oarsman's habitual mental atrophy, the adviser's early decision to develop his mind had resulted in the growth of important intellectual character traits and a number of valuable thinking skills. Still bleary-eyed from being woken up from a dead sleep, the adviser's mental autopilot alone was capable of meeting the challenge. With apparent effortlessness, the adviser asked the right questions (thanks to his intellectual curiosity), continued digging for information until he had what he needed (intellectual tenacity), ensured that he had all the facts the king might require and that those facts were correct (intellectual carefulness), evaluated the relative importance of the information being accumulated (critical thinking), and finally anticipated and resolved the potential fallout from this new information (problem solving). The adviser didn't have to invest in multiple trips or be at the peak of mental alertness; his intellectual character (and the thinking skills that resulted from that character) more than made up for the unfavorable circumstances.

Intellectual character is not easily acquired. It requires a real thirst for truth and a willingness to work hard in that pursuit. However, as we put in the effort and over time begin to develop intellectually virtuous habits, the rewards are life changing. We grow in knowledge (with all the benefits to our lives that that brings). And, we become better thinkers (allowing us to unlock the tremendous potential of our knowledge and of the thinking process itself). But as valuable as these things are, the most important benefits that result from an increase in intellectually virtuous character are still to come.

LOVING GOD

"Love the Lord your God with all your heart and
with all your soul and with all your mind and with all
your strength. . . . Love your neighbor as yourself."
There is no commandment greater than these.

MARK 12:30-31

So far we have looked primarily at the benefits intellectual character produces in our own lives. And, as long as our aim continues to be the truth (and not simply the fruits of truth), there is nothing wrong with that. In fact, the message of the parable of the talents is clear—to the extent that we are good stewards of our God-given gifts, God wants us to enjoy the fruit of our efforts. But this raises an important question. What does it mean to be a good steward of our talents? I believe Jesus gives us the answer. In his response to the Pharisee's question about which commandment was the greatest, Jesus replied, "'Love the Lord your God with all your heart and with all your soul and with all your mind and with all your strength. . . . Love your neighbor as yourself.' There is no commandment greater than these" (Mark 12:30-31). In other words, everything we do in life—including the stewardship of our intellectual gifts—needs to be assessed by the extent to which it helps us honor God and serve our neighbor.

As a Christian, I have come to believe that growing in intellectual virtue is inseparable from following the two greatest commandments. Indeed, far and away the most exciting benefits that come from growth in intellectual character are found when we turn our eyes away from ourselves and toward God and our neighbor.

INTELLECTUAL CHARACTER AND WORSHIP

Although there is much more to it than an attitude of adoration, our ability to enter into worship and the depth of our worship are both closely tied to the character of our minds. Worship is not the practice of artificially conjuring up feelings about nothing in particular. Throughout the Scriptures, worship is consistently and explicitly rooted in knowledge. As David writes, "When I *consider* your heavens, the work of your fingers, the moon and the stars, which you have set in place, what is mankind that you are mindful of them?" (Psalm 8:3-4, italics mine). "LORD, our Lord," he says, "how majestic is your name in all the earth!" (Psalm 8:1). The close link between our ability to worship and knowledge is also found throughout the Prophets. As Isaiah writes, "Do you not know? Have you not heard? Has it not been told you from the beginning? Have you not understood . . . ? The LORD is the everlasting God, the Creator of the ends of the earth" (Isaiah 40:21, 28). Simply put, to the extent that we have applied our minds to understanding God and his world, our ability to worship him increases.

This is an inadequate analogy on a number of levels, but consider the difference between the following compliments given to a novelist by two otherwise equally intelligent fans. Fan number one, who had skimmed the book while watching Letterman, comments, "Yeah, umm, I thought it was really good, especially the part about history. That was cool." In contrast, the second fan, who had read hundreds of well-regarded novels (including this one twice) is both enthusiastic and substantial: "I think this might be the best novel I have ever read," she says. "Your use of historical analogy gave the story tremendous depth as well as creating a sense of foreboding more ominous than any novel in recent memory. I also thought that your insights into the causes of the Great Depression throughout the novel were genuinely compelling. Thank you." Both compliments were probably well meant, and yet the comments made by fan number two are clearly in another category. Unlike the trite and almost meaningless remarks made by fan number one, the second set of comments reflects an earnest desire to understand the novel and demonstrate an appropriate adoration of the novel's virtues. If you were the novelist, which set of compliments would mean the most to you?

Christian worship, of course, is more than just knowing a lot of information about God. It is also profoundly and intimately relational. The psalmist expresses this beautifully when he writes,

You have searched me, LORD,
    and you know me.
You know when I sit and when I rise;
    you perceive my thoughts from afar.
You discern my going out and my lying down;
    you are familiar with all my ways.
Before a word is on my tongue
    you, LORD, know it completely. . . .
I praise you because I am fearfully and wonderfully made;
    your works are wonderful,
I know that full well. . . .
    Search me, God, and know my heart. (Psalm 139:1-4, 14, 23)

And as Paul writes to Timothy, "I know whom I have believed, and am convinced that he is able" (2 Timothy 1:12). Clearly

Christian worship is relational, but just as clearly, that loving relationship deepens and grows only in parallel with our knowledge of God. For, as Thomas Aquinas observed, "Love follows knowledge."[1]

But doesn't this knowledge of God come supernaturally, through the Holy Spirit? And if so, doesn't that mean that intellectual character is irrelevant to our worship of God? If there is anything that comes through clearly in both Scripture and the history of the church, it is that those who have had the deepest and most intimate relationships with God were those who, far from sitting passively, pursued God with everything that they were—including their minds. There is no more important evidence of this than in the statement from Jesus that introduced this chapter. What is the greatest commandment? "Love the Lord your God with all your heart and with all your soul and with *all your mind* and with all your strength" (Mark 12:30-31, italics mine). Both our worship and our relationship with God demand that our minds be fully engaged.

Before we move on, it is also important to recognize that for Christians the earnest pursuit of truth and a commitment to being the best stewards of our minds as we can be are in themselves authentic acts of worship. When Paul famously appealed to the early Christians to "offer [their] bodies as a living sacrifice, holy and pleasing to God" (Romans 12:1), the point he was making was that our lives—in their entirety—are meant for God's glory. Therefore, to the extent that we are being good stewards of our bodies (and our minds), we are participating in an act of worship. Conversely, when we are lazy or apathetic in our pursuit of the truth, or squander the intellectual potential we have (no matter how limited we may think it to be), we are showing contempt for the one we are seeking to honor. As C. S. Lewis put it, "God is no fonder of intellectual slackers than of any other slackers."[2] In short, not only is seeking to understand God and his creation in itself an act of worship, but as we grow in that knowledge, our explicit acts of worship will increasingly and more completely express his glory.

INTELLECTUAL CHARACTER AND CHRISTIAN APOLOGETICS

So far we have seen that as Christians grow in intellectual character, they will usually experience a corresponding increase in the quality of both their worship and their relationship with God. That alone is enough reason to pursue a genuinely transformed mind. But the growth of intellectual character includes other spiritually important benefits as well. The intellectually virtuous Christian, for instance, will also bring increasing honor to God in the public sphere through a progressively more powerful apologetic for their faith. Think of it as the E. F. Hutton principle applied to our faith. As a natural byproduct of their consistent and earnest pursuit of the truth, intellectually virtuous Christians will not be easily intimidated or threatened by arguments that might have otherwise undermined their faith and the potential faith of those listening. Instead, thanks to their command of the evidence and their sharply tuned thinking skills, they will be able to clearly and persuasively defend their faith against all comers. That doesn't mean every intellectually virtuous Christian will be another C. S. Lewis or G. K. Chesterton. However, it does mean that as Christians take the stewardship of their minds seriously, they will be increasingly able, as Peter commands, "to give an answer to everyone who asks you to give the reason for the hope that you have" (1 Peter 3:15).

But apologetics is not just a matter of creating clever and well-supported arguments. Who we are is often more important than what we say, and this leads to the next important byproduct of intellectual character in the life of the Christian. When we take on godly characteristics in our thinking (and this is what the intellectual virtues are), our actions also come to reflect God's goodness.

This is hardly surprising. We take it for granted that our ideas wield considerable influence over our actions; and, therefore, it makes sense that an increase in the virtue of our thinking is likely to have a positive influence on our behavior. For instance, if you begin to treat my opinions in a fair-minded way, it is only natural that your actual behavior toward me will also grow increasingly gracious. Conversely, history is full of examples, such as Hitler's Germany, where contemptuous ideas about a group of people gave rise to unspeakably cruel behavior. The point is simple and powerful. How we think influences how we behave. Without developing some form of intellectual schizophrenia, it is nearly impossible for us to grow in intellectual character without seeing positive changes in our behavior; and as our behavior grows increasingly loving and good, we will draw people to the Author of love and goodness.

INTELLECTUAL CHARACTER AND HONORING
GOD THROUGH EXCELLENCE

At the core of Christian faith is the assumption that God is perfectly good, perfectly loving, perfectly just—the standard of excellence in all things. Also at the center of our faith is the conviction that although we are sinful, we are to aspire (with the help of the Holy Spirit) to be like God. As Peter points out, God commands Christians to "be holy, because I am holy" (1 Peter 1:16). Or as Paul states in 1 Corinthians, "Follow my example, as I follow the example of Christ" (1 Corinthians 11:1). Therefore, when we are successful in achieving intellectual excellence, we are bringing honor to God—the author and perfect embodiment of reason and truth. Of course, the reverse is equally true. As Andreas Köstenberger writes regarding the Christian obligation to pursue intellectual excellence, "Mediocrity and sloppy workmanship never glorify God."[3]

In this chapter we have seen that the pursuit of intellectual character is directly linked to the health of our spiritual lives. Our ability to worship, the quality of our relationship to God and our role in influencing how others view God are all rooted in the depth and breadth of our understanding of God and his world resulting from virtuous intellectual character. In addition, our growing knowledge base and the increasingly sharp thinking skills that come from intellectual character are also critical in our ability to persuasively defend our faith. Finally, intellectual character is an essential ingredient in our moral development. This partial list demonstrates that, far from being some worldly abstraction, growing in intellectual character is profoundly practical and directly relevant to our aim as Christians to love God completely.

LOVING YOUR NEIGHBOR

---

*Love the Lord your God with all your heart and with all
your soul and with all your mind and with all your strength.
The second is this: Love your neighbor as yourself.*

MARK 12:30-31

THERE IS A WHOLE HOST OF WAYS in which intellectual character is foundational to loving our neighbor as ourselves. Most of these are as important as they are obvious. Let's start with what may be the most straightforward connection between intellectual character and loving one another. The intellectually virtuous person is more likely to make wise decisions and, therefore, is less likely to bring pain and suffering on others. For instance, the well-meaning father who loses most of his family's savings by investing in Costa Rican real estate without having ever been to the country, and with minimal knowledge of the deal's legal small print, does not hurt just himself by his reckless and hasty decision making. In the same way, the newspaper reporter who, based on some casual office gossip, writes an article recklessly suggesting the imminent demise of a major bank doesn't have only his own reputation to answer for.

In contrast, the wise decision-making processes of intellectually virtuous people usually produce benefits that spread well beyond their immediate context. Prudent choices by a business executive secure not only his own economic well-being but the jobs and financial stability of all those who work for the company. The scientist who refuses to be rushed into prematurely approving a new nutritional supplement for the market is protecting both the good of the company she works for and the lives and well-being of thousands of consumers and their families. And we could go on and on. Simply put, to the degree that we become people of intellectual character, we also grow in our ability to make decisions that bring good to others. In this way, intellectual character is an essential ingredient in loving others.

The first few illustrations we have looked at strongly hint at another important way in which intellectual character is tied to loving our neighbor—that is, the indispensible role it plays in creating trust between people. In the Oscar-nominated film *A Simple Plan* (1998), two brothers and an old friend from a rural American town stumble upon a small plane crashed in a remote wood. When they investigate the crash and find a single dead body with no identification and several bags containing millions of dollars, a plan is hatched to conceal their discovery and keep the money for themselves. This decision to deceive their friends and family thus initiates a chain of lies that slowly leads to the unraveling of trust within their small town, destroys one of their marriages and creates a wall of suspicion between the friends that climaxes in the murder of one and the assisted suicide of another.

It's not exactly a feel-good Hallmark classic. Nevertheless, as well as any in recent memory, the movie does illustrate both the fundamental role that trust plays in creating healthy and happy relationships and the destructive effects that a lack of trust can have on those relationships. When the friends in *A Simple Plan* made the decision to hide the truth, they not only began building a wall between themselves and their community, but they demonstrated to each other (and to themselves) that they were untrustworthy people. Viewing everyone else through the lenses of their own lack of intellectual virtue had made them unable to trust others. The important lesson is this: to the degree that we disregard the pursuit of truth in our own lives, we forfeit the ability to trust others, and when this happens we have fundamentally undermined our ability to love one another. As the movie demonstrated, this is not some irrelevant abstraction. The consequences of a breakdown in trust resulting from a lack of intellectual character are about as real and painful as anything we will experience in life.

Beyond the consistent practice of telling the truth, there are a number of other ways that the intellectually virtuous person helps to build trust. To begin with, as we have already seen, the intellectually virtuous person will become a good listener. Intellectual curiosity (wanting to know more), humility (openness to other perspectives because we know we don't have all the answers), fair-mindedness (wanting to give other ideas a fair assessment), and carefulness (wanting to make sure we accurately understand the other person) all encourage better listening. When we take on these character traits and start to really listen to people, we not only gain in our understanding of the truth (and about the people we are listening to), but we communicate that we value both them and their ideas. This process dignifies them, demonstrates to them that their ideas are in good hands and, therefore, establishes the foundation for a healthy relationship.

Intellectual character also builds trust by increasing the likelihood that we will get our facts right. Let's say your car is acting up and you take it to a local mechanic. The mechanic reports a problem in the exhaust and, upon your authorization, replaces the muffler. Unfortunately, a day later the old problem resurfaces and you take the car back in. This time the mechanic says that your air filter is the problem and replaces it at further cost. Another two days pass, and yet again the same sounds and sputtering are back. Getting things wrong once could have been an honest mistake, but when it happens again you begin to suspect more malicious forces may be at work. Whether it is incompetence or blatant dishonesty, the cost of the errors to you in dollars and the effect on the relationship in increasing mistrust are the same. Simply put, when we are consistently wrong about things, people stop listening to us and the death of relationships is not far off.

It is also important to note that it matters little whether or not the mechanic was sincere. As J. P. Moreland has observed, "I can believe with all my might that my car will fly me to Hawaii . . . but that fervency doesn't change a thing. . . . What matters is not how sincere I am in believing [something] but whether or not the belief is true."[1] In contrast to the harmful effects that erroneous knowledge can have on our relationships, the intellectual virtues are a critical component in building life-enhancing and healthy, trusting relationships because they are primarily about getting things right.

The trust that comes from intellectually virtuous character can be fragile initially, but as it grows it can develop a momentum of its own that can infuse the relational culture of families and social networks with mirth and life-giving dynamism. Compare the healthy family dynamics seen on the 1980s sitcom *The Cosby Show* with those paraded on *The Jerry Springer Show* today. In most cases, the sense of contentment and mutual support seen in the Huxtable family and the angry suspicion present on *Jerry Springer* can both be traced back to the relative levels of intellectual character that exist within the respective families. Significantly, the level of trust found in families does not cease to matter when family members step out the front door. Trusting families help produce healthy and thriving communities, and families dominated by intellectual vice support the growth of suspicion and cynicism in those communities. To the extent that an entire culture internalizes intellectually virtuous values, the trust that results can transform a society.

Empirical evidence seems to bear this out. Max Weber famously argued that the material prosperity of the Protestant nations was ultimately rooted in a set of values that, among other things, extended the trust necessary for thriving commerce beyond the family and out to the larger society.[2] The father of the sociology of science, Robert Merton, has made a similar argument concerning the link between the intellectual culture of Protestantism and the growth of science in the sixteenth and seventeenth centuries.[3] More recently, a number of highly respected scholars have linked trust-engendering intellectual values to a number of outcomes, including the flourishing of democracy, economic growth and a lack of corruption. These studies confirm on a national level the intuitive link that many of us have made between well-being in personal and familial relationships and intellectual virtue.[4]

There is no question that intellectually virtuous people will be more successful in building trust between themselves and others than will their nonvirtuous counterparts. There is also no question that without this trust it is nearly impossible to love our neighbor in any meaningful way. But there are also a number of other ways in which intellectual character is directly linked to the practical love of our neighbor.

In the life of Dr. Paul Brand we have already seen how intellectual character can lead to breakthroughs that can help to end the suffering of others. Paul Brand returned to India because of his faith-inspired love of the nation's people, but this love (on its own) was powerless in providing practical medical treatment for the country's large leper community. No matter how deeply he might have felt for those suffering with leprosy, it was not until his intellectual character kicked in that Dr. Brand's medical breakthroughs became possible. The leper community no doubt appreciated the sympathy that Brand and others felt for their condition, but it was the incisive questions he raised (intellectual curiosity) and his diligence in sticking with the questions until he got answers (intellectual tenacity) that provided practical solutions for their suffering. As it was in Dr. Brand's case, intellectual character is often the difference between well-meaning but impotent feelings and life-transforming expressions of practical love.

In the chapter "The Benefits of Knowing More About More," we saw how the increase in knowledge that invariably follows a person with virtuous thinking habits can open up for him or her an increasingly rich and fulfilling world. When we turn our attention to loving our neighbor, we find this same principle at work. As an undergraduate at Trinity Western University, I had the chance to take a class from Paul Chamberlain. Philosophy was not the most popular major at Trinity, and Dr. Chamberlain was not the head of the philosophy faculty, but these things didn't seem to matter. His classes were almost always packed to capacity. The reason for the popularity of his classes was rooted in his intellectual character. Dr. Chamberlain loved the truth, and that passion for understanding not only made his world rich and satisfying, but it poured out onto everyone he came in contact with. We flooded into his classes because his own intellectual character was opening up to us a larger and more fulfilling world. Take a second to think back on all the teachers, books, or even friends and acquaintances whose knowledge and love of the truth have transformed your life for the better. I am willing to bet a great deal (metaphorically, of course) that the people behind these life-enhancing truths were almost inevitably people of unusually virtuous intellectual character.

Because truth is at the core of the noble life, standing up for the truth in difficult circumstances can also call others to a greater awareness of their own potential and of their own God-given dignity. I had the privilege of growing up in Kenya as the son of missionaries during the 1980s. At this time, Kenya was becoming increasingly authoritarian, and speaking out publicly against the government carried with it the risk of imprisonment or worse. At the peak of the political oppression, the thoughtful and soft-spoken pastor of my church got up one Sunday and preached a sermon that drew direct parallels between the complaints of the Old Testament prophets and the practices of the Kenyan government. It was not a flashy sermon, but the congregation sat absolutely stunned, aware that the young pastor was risking his life by speaking what he believed to be God's truth. Sure enough, within hours of the sermon the pastor, Mutava Musyimi, was forced into hiding. From that point on, he and other evangelical pastors in Nairobi willing to criticize the government were increasingly harassed and threatened, but in the end, their courage helped unleash a movement that ultimately led to the nation's first genuinely multiparty elections in 1992 and, later, the nation's first peaceful transition of power in 2002.[5]

By putting his allegiance to the truth and his concern for the good of his country ahead of himself, Mutava Musyimi helped bring new freedoms to the Kenyan people. But his courage was also loving in another important way. By taking the stand he did, the young pastor made it difficult for others to sit passively on the sidelines. His words and ideas were a direct challenge to his countrymen to honor the truth, and for those who took up his challenge, it was a considerable step toward the development of intellectually virtuous character in their own lives. When virtuous thinking leads us to act virtuously, we are issuing a loving appeal to our neighbor to join us in this good and God-honoring quest.

During the Cold War, a Czech dissident named Václav Havel spoke out consistently and courageously for freedom in the face of Soviet oppression. This courage helped produce what became known as the Velvet Revolution against the Soviet Union in 1989, which signaled the end of the Cold War. When the Czech Republic gained its independence in 1993, the people honored Havel's intellectual courage by making him the nation's first president. In closing, I cannot resist including portions of a story he wrote at the height of Communist oppression that poignantly illustrates the principle we also saw in Mutava Musyimi's life. Here I will quote Havel at length.

> The manager of a fruit-and-vegetable shop places in his window, among the onions and carrots, the slogan: "Workers of the world, unite!" Why does he do it? . . .
>
> That poster was delivered to our greengrocer from the enterprise headquarters along with the onions and the carrots. He put them all into the window simply because it has been done that way for years, because everyone does it, and because that is the way it has to be. If he were to refuse, there could be trouble. . . .
>
> Let us now imagine that one day something in our greengrocer snaps and he stops putting up the slogans merely to ingratiate himself. He stops voting in elections he knows are a farce. He begins to say what he really thinks at political meetings. . . . He discovers once more his suppressed identity and dignity. He gives his freedom a concrete significance. His revolt is an attempt to live within the truth.
>
> The bill is not long in coming. He will be relieved of his post as manager of the shop and transferred to the warehouse. His pay will be reduced. His hopes for a holiday in Bulgaria will evaporate. His children's access to higher education will be threatened. His superiors will harass him and his fellow workers will wonder about him. . . .
>
> [And why? Because] the greengrocer has not committed a

simple, individual offense, isolated in its own uniqueness, but something incomparably more serious. . . . He has shattered the world of appearances. . . . He has said the emperor is naked. And because the emperor is in fact naked, something extremely dangerous has happened: by his action, the green-grocer has addressed the world.[6]

It may seem less dramatic than the case of Mutava Musyimi in Kenya, or the greengrocer in Communist Czechoslovakia, but when a child stands up for truth against peer pressure in the school playground, and when the employee humbly but firmly challenges unethical practices by her company, their decisions are an equally powerful and loving challenge to their neighbor to think and act within the truth. Until we take up this challenge to "live within the truth," it will be difficult for us to fulfill our purpose of loving God and our neighbor.

Over the last four chapters we have looked at a number of the rewards that come to us as we grow in intellectual character. We have seen that the intellectually virtuous person will always grow in knowledge and that this increase in knowledge carries with it a host of life-changing benefits. We have also seen that the pursuit of truth invariably sharpens the way we think—that is, our thinking skills are honed, and in the process we become heirs to a second set of rewards. But these pleasant byproducts of intel-lectual virtue only gain their ultimate significance when they are understood in light of Jesus' commandment to love God and our neighbor. As we looked at the benefits of intellectual character in light of this ultimate purpose, we found that, far from being an irrelevant abstraction, intellectual character is inseparable from loving God and loving each other. By this point we have a pretty good idea of both what intellectual character is and the many benefits that will come to us as we grow in virtue. But how do we do it? How do we go about becoming people who love God with all our minds (that is, people of virtuous intellectual character)? The remainder of this book is an attempt to give us some practical tools we can use as we embark on the God-honoring quest for virtuous intellectual character.

courage

carefulness

tenacity

fair-mindedness

curiosity

honesty

humility

BECOMING PEOPLE OF INTELLECTUAL CHARACTER

Developing Virtuous Intellectual Character

When you start mathematics you do not begin
with calculus; you begin with simple addition.

C. S. Lewis, *Mere Christianity*

We have spent quite a bit of time looking at what intellectual character is and its profound influence on our lives. We have seen that developing virtuous intellectual character doesn't just affect traditionally academic pursuits but pours out into every part of our experience, transforming our lives as it does. But so far we have only hinted at how we can become people of good intellectual character. While the road to personal transformation is rarely a neat series of concrete steps, there are some basic principles and practices that, if consistently lived out, will prove invaluable on our journey.

Step 1: Eyes on the Prize

Our ability to stick with the project of intellectual character formation will be directly proportional to the value we place on the prize waiting for us at the end. Along with the writer of Proverbs, we must believe that understanding is "more precious than rubies" and that "nothing you desire can compare with her" (Proverbs 3:15). That is simply fundamental. The transformation of our intellectual character is no small thing. It is not something that happens overnight, nor is it something that comes without significant cost. It requires both longevity and a willingness to persevere when the going gets tough. Unless we see how important truth and intellectual character are to our lives, when things get difficult our good intentions are likely to fade into hazy sentimentality or the cynicism of failure.

Imagine two equally talented Brazilian boys growing up with the dream of playing in the World Cup. Edson plays primarily because he loves the game. Give him some free time, and he is out in the streets juggling his soccer ball or practicing free kicks in pickup games with his buddies. The other boy, Gilberto, wants to play in the World Cup primarily because of his desire to be famous. He too spends his free time playing soccer in the streets, but mainly because he knows that the girls will be watching and that his skills have earned him the admiration of his peers.

As they grow up, both boys get picked to be part of their local club team, but when casual games turn to rigorous training, complete with hours of repetitive drills, sprints and hill climbs, and with no guarantee of external success, both boys are tempted to give up. For Gilberto, the decision to quit is a relatively easy one. For him soccer was always just a means to fame and popularity, and there are easier, less painful ways to achieve these things. On the other hand, Edson plays because he loves soccer. Yes, he dreams of playing for his country, and maybe even getting the wealth and fame that that would bring, but when you boil it down to its essence, he plays because he loves the game—for itself. The drills may get tedious at times, and the physical exertion might bring him to the point of collapse, but he is doing what he loves. In Edson's mind, there couldn't have been an easier choice. The costs, if you can even call them costs, are simply a part of the joy he experiences as a growing and improving soccer player. The same principle applies to our thinking habits. If we love the truth, we will handle the trials of intellectual character development with grace. Indeed, the trials will seem like a trifle to us compared with the prize that awaits us at the end.

While it is a little more complicated, there is a conceivable scenario that is worth mentioning in which Gilberto might still develop a passionate love for the game and the character that often accompanies this sort of love. Let's say Gilberto comes to the conclusion that, outside of soccer, there is literally no other chance for him to achieve the wealth and fame he longs for so desperately. In this case, although he dreads the physical agony and tedium of soccer practices, he might still stick with it. Because he lacks the spark that Edson brings to the field, everything will be harder for Gilberto and his progress will likely be slower. Yet, because he perseveres, he does see his skill and fitness levels grow. Eventually he manages to get into a game and manages to score the winning goal to the universal praise of the club's fans. The acclaim he receives spurs him on further, and as he works harder and improves further still, slowly he comes to see beauty and joy in the game he began playing for ulterior motives. It doesn't look virtuous, and it is fragile, but what we have here might still become the seeds of character formation. Significantly, Gilberto's less noble path to character is probably more like the path many of us will take toward intellectual character. It is not the honorable path, and it certainly is not the easiest, but few of us start off with minds guided by an untainted love of truth and intellectual virtue.

However, it is important to remember that even in Gilberto's case the foundation of character transformation remained a love for the thing itself—in this case soccer. In the same way, the foundation for the growth of intellectual character is found in developing a love for truth. Which leads to the million-dollar question: How do we cultivate a love for truth? To some the question itself is absurd. Aren't we naturally curious, seekers of truth? Current educational philosophy in America rests on the assumption that as long as you give people a safe opportunity to learn, they will naturally bloom into lifelong lovers of truth. There is an element of truth to this view. God has created us in his image, with the ability to revel in truth and creativity. All of us have felt the natural rush that comes when we discover some new and interesting piece of information or the joy that comes when we piece together fragments of knowledge in order to create a new and life-giving insight.

But according to Scripture that is only half of the story. There is also a part of us that has set itself against God's goodness and truth. And reality provides chilling confirmation of our natural gravitation toward deceit and lies. There are times when we not only don't love the truth but we don't even want to love the truth. Unfortunately, the love of truth—the very cornerstone upon which intellectual character is built—is not something that will grow freely and naturally if left unattended. It must be cultivated. So it's back to the beginning: How do we cultivate the love for truth?

Step 2: Cultivating a Love for Truth

For some of us the process of cultivating a love for the truth may begin by simply making the decision to love the truth. Others of us, not even wanting but still acknowledging the importance of the truth, may need to begin by wanting to want the truth. It sounds flippant, but even that mustard seed of motivation can be enough to begin the transformation of our minds.

Being discerning in what we choose to think about is a critical way to begin cultivating a love for truth. As the apostle Paul stated, "Whatever is true, whatever is noble, whatever is right . . . think about such things" (Philippians 4:8). There are a couple of reasons why this is so important. First, our thinking guides our behavior. As Dallas Willard says, "Whatever occupies our mind very largely governs what we do."[1] Second, and more directly related to developing good intellectual character, is the fact that when we dwell on goodness and truth, we are much more likely to see the consequences of truth.

Simply taking the time to consider the results of being tenacious or fair-minded in our thinking can be a tremendous encouragement to us in our quest for character because it reminds us of the goodness that awaits us at the end. A parallel can be drawn to our example of the Brazilian Gilberto. He came to love soccer, not because he initially loved it for its own sake, as Edson did, but because he had tasted the fruit of success in soccer. It was only then that he gradually came to love the game for itself. What are some of the fruits of being intellectually courageous, or humble, or careful? Take a few minutes to write down all the positive effects that would be seen in your job or family life if your thinking were consistently honest, careful, fair or tenacious.

Very closely related to the importance of thinking about the fruits of intellectual character is the value of spending time with those who already model many of the intellectual virtues. Who do you know that strikes you as a good example of intellectual character? Can you think of people in your life who seem to treat the ideas of others with respect, who are always asking good questions and seem to weigh their words carefully? If so, what good things seem to come to them as a result of these intellectual character traits? Not only does spending time with people who love truth give us a taste of the fruits of intellectual character, but it can give us a glimpse of what intellectual virtue looks like when it is lived out and, therefore, how we might begin to establish patterns of good thinking in our own lives.

STEP 3: HONESTLY EVALUATING OUR
OWN THINKING HABITS

If the most important step in developing praiseworthy intellectual character is cultivating a deep love of truth, an almost equally critical step is coming to the sober recognition that our intellectual character is deeply flawed. Shining an honestly critical light on our intellectual character is never fun, and in many cases it can be downright painful. For many people the fear of confronting their failings is enough to end the quest for character before it begins. Yet until we see our failings and their ugly consequences, we will not feel the need for change. In this regard our culture does us no favors. Our penchant for rationalizing evil and downplaying flaws for the sake of self-esteem frustrates honest self-critique and acts to undermine intellectual character in society at large. Like the children in Lake Wobegon, Minnesota, virtually all of us see ourselves as having intellectual character that is "above average."[2]

This is not to say that we are all intellectually bankrupt, and it is certainly not to say we are beyond intellectual redemption. Not at all. It is to say that there is a good likelihood that we are not nearly as intellectually virtuous as we would like to believe ourselves to be; and that unless we get to the truth about our character, we will have no chance of growing into the thinkers that God wants us to be. So how can we start this initially painful self-assessment?

One suggestion is to go back and to look at the definitions of the intellectual virtues described in this book and then consider how closely the description of that virtue fits you in your work and leisure. Don't settle for general impressions. Any self-assessment that does not consider specific examples of the virtue or vice in your life will be unhelpful. I might even suggest you try assigning yourself a rating of one to ten on each of the seven virtues. When I was a teacher at Rosslyn Academy in Kenya, I used to give my students a self-assessment rating form.[3] When they had rated themselves on each of the virtues, I then asked them to write down several examples of either virtue or vice in each area, after which they were encouraged to re-evaluate their earlier self-assessment. Most of the time, our initial impressions of our intellectual character do not hold up under closer scrutiny.

Before you make a final assessment of your own character, a second helpful suggestion might be to reconsider your own intellectual character in light of those people that you deem to be role models of one virtue or another—the more virtuous the person, the more helpful this suggestion can be. Many times holding up the candle of an ideal to our own character can betray flaws that would have remained hidden in the dark.

Before we go any further, it is important to remember that the point of this honest self-assessment is not self-defeating demoralization—something that would only discourage us from pursuing personal intellectual growth. This entire book is based on the premise that God loves us infinitely and has created us in his image, with a good purpose and plan for our lives. His good news through Jesus is that despite our failings and flaws we can still become the people he wants us to be. But just as in our spiritual salvation, where we will never be able to receive God's grace until we see our need for it, we will never begin to love God with our minds until we see the depravity of our intellectual character. The good news begins by looking honestly at the bad news.

STEP 4: WHAT'S THE PLAN, STAN?

Once we have confronted the deep flaws in our intellectual character, acknowledged our need for fundamental personal change and begun to wake up to the life-giving goodness of truth, the next important step in becoming better people—intellectually—is the creation of a plan for nurturing intellectual character development in our lives. "Projects of personal transformation rarely, if ever, succeed by accident," writes Dallas Willard. "Imagine a person wondering day after day if they are going to learn Arabic . . . just waiting to see whether it would 'happen.' That would be laughable." Willard continues, if you want to learn Arabic "you will need to sign up for language courses, listen to recordings, buy books, associate with people who speak Arabic, immerse yourself in the culture, possibly spend some intensive time in Jordan or Morocco and practice, practice, practice."4 The transformation of our intellectual character requires the same sort of action plan.

STEP 5: MAPPING OUT OUR USE OF TIME

The first important step in the action plan toward intellectual character can feel like a bit of a downer. This is the process of sitting down, perhaps with a few close friends or your spouse, and analyzing your life as it relates to the mind. How is your intellect used at work—or how should it be used, ideally? Are there areas of work where intellectual character is required? What traits in particular are needed? And, how well have you fared in those areas when you have been tested? How do you use your free time? Are your leisure activities conducive or detrimental to intellectual growth? One of the most instructive questions we can ask ourselves is, what do we do with free time when we are on autopilot? What is our default mental activity (or would nonactivity be more accurate)? TV? Video games? Even consider apparently unconnected concerns like your eating, sleeping and fitness habits. Are you taking good care of your body? Ignoring you body can have direct and negative consequences on mental alertness, which, in turn, can sabotage the growth of intellectual character.

It is hard to overestimate the importance of a thorough and critical analysis of your lifestyle to your quest for intellectual character. For starters, a thorough critique uncovers the habit patterns that dominate (and often enslave) us. Most of us do not wake up and say, "Today my goal is to cut corners on my assignment at work and then lazily waste my leisure time watching mind-numbing reruns of *The Price is Right.*" That we end up doing these things is usually not a conscious choice but a result of the harmful habit patterns we have let develop over time. A critical survey of our lifestyle creates an awareness of how pervasive our intellectually bad habits are, and suggests ways in which we can begin to change these habit patterns.

Another important realization many of us will come to as a result of a critical self-assessment is that our lives are often weighed down by details attached to misguided priorities. For instance, some friends of mine—whom I otherwise respect a great deal—love watching television. And while there is nothing wrong with quality TV in moderation, they devote a considerable portion of their time and energy not just to watching TV but to a host of related activities. They scour newspapers and the net double-checking the times for their many favorite shows. Because they cannot possibly watch all these shows each night, they then spend additional time programming their digital box to record whatever their normal viewing will force them to miss. Finally, if there is any time left in the day, they often spend it flipping through magazines or websites devoted to television, or to the actors who star on television. In other words, it is not just the decision to watch an excessive amount of television that is the problem. Equally destructive to their hopes for personal growth are the apparently endless, and usually pointless, activities attached to their TV habit. If we want to develop our minds, one of the first things we must do is to carve out time for intellectually rewarding pursuits by simplifying our lives.

STEP 6: ACCOUNTABILITY

A further likely outcome of any honest self-critique is the realization that in order to overcome the power of ingrained intellectual habit patterns we will need backup. No matter how committed we are to becoming people of good intellectual character, there will be times when the power of our habits will feel insurmountable. It is at these moments that the encouragement of trusted friends can make all the difference. For at least a couple of reasons the very act of having others take part in your lifestyle assessment can be a useful starting point in creating this needed accountability. That person, or group of people, already knows what your goal is and what habit patterns you will need to overcome. It is also likely that you chose the people you did both because they are sympathetic to your intellectual aims and because you can trust them.

Accountability groups can take a variety of forms. Deciding to take a stimulating course together at your local church or community college can be a great hub around which to build an intellectual accountability group. A book club is also a great way to mix intellectual growth with the joys of growing relationships. The point is that intellectual accountability can be fun and socially enriching as well as intellectually challenging. But whatever you choose to do by way of accountability, the ultimate aim of the group should be the self-conscious replacement of old, negative thinking habits with positive new ones.

STEP 7: SPREADING THE WORD

Another possible component of an action plan for the development of intellectual virtue is to talk to others about intellectual virtue. Any preacher or teacher will tell you that nothing challenges personal growth more than the act of telling others about it. When we talk to others about the importance of intellectual character, we not only develop our understanding of it further, but we are reminded of the gap between who we aim to be and who we are. As we grow, it will also serve as a source of encouragement when we see how far we have come.

STEP 8: FINDING HEROES

Seeking out heroes can also be an important component of intellectual transformation. It is not just children who can benefit from inspirational role models. If accountability groups encourage us to stay the course when the going is tough, intellectual heroes serve to inspire in us a vision of what we might become. From Aristotle to C. S. Lewis, those who have written extensively about character transformation have pointed to the power of imitation in the initial stages of character formation. Lewis called the phenomenon *pretending into being*. "There are two kinds of pretending," says Lewis. "There is the bad kind, where the pretense is there instead of the real thing; as when a man pretends he is going to help you instead of really helping you. But there is also a good kind, where the pretense leads to the real thing." He continues, "Very often the only way to get a quality in reality is to start behaving as if you had it already. That's why children's games are so important. They are always pretending to be grown-ups—playing soldiers, playing shop. But all the time, they are hardening their muscles and sharpening their wits, so that the pretense of being grown-up helps them to grow up in earnest."[5]

STEP 9: WE MUST ACT

If we hope to develop virtuous intellectual character, we must choose to act. William James, one of the greatest minds America has ever produced, was absolutely spot-on when he said, "No matter how full a reservoir of maxims one may possess, and no matter how good one's sentiments may be, if one has not taken advantage of every concrete opportunity to *act*, one's character may remain entirely unaffected for the better."[6]

STEP 10: START SMALL

But where do we start? How can we begin to act in virtuous ways when the habits and ruts that make up our intellectual character currently lead us away from good character, not toward it? Start small. Like the marathon runner who begins to develop her physical stamina by running half a mile a day, the first step toward improving your intellectual character should be reasonably achievable. Go back and take a look at the evaluation you have done of your thinking habits. Then pick one choice you consistently make that undermines good thinking habits, and attack it. Just because it seems small, this action on your part is far from insignificant. In fact the reality is just the opposite, for it is in these seemingly unimportant everyday choices that the battle is won or lost. So when you are tired and tempted to switch on the TV or surf the net, decide to open a book for a few minutes. When you are tempted to ignore a newspaper article because it will require too much mental energy, or because it appears to contradict your opinion, take the ten minutes required to read it thoughtfully. Be heroic in the little things, said William James, so that "when the hour of dire need draws nigh, it may find you not unnerved and untrained to stand the test."[7]

13

SEVEN SUGGESTIONS FOR
EDUCATORS AND PARENTS

Intelligence plus character—that is the goal of true education.

MARTIN LUTHER KING JR.,
IN *THE WORDS OF MARTIN LUTHER KING JR.*

IN THIS BOOK I HAVE ATTEMPTED TO SHOW how profoundly our intellectual character influences our everyday lives. Among other things, we have seen that our thinking habits shape the quality of our personal relationships, the success of our work, the depth of our spiritual lives and even the fulfillment we can get out of our leisure activities. Wherever we go and whatever we do the quality of our intellectual character matters.

However, there is one area where the character of our minds holds particular significance, and that is education. True education is not limited to the classroom. As all parents know, it is present wherever we are earnestly seeking to understand the world around us. Nevertheless, our success as lifelong learners is particularly influenced by the thinking patterns that we develop in the two principal greenhouses of intellectual character—the home and the classroom. What follows are seven practical suggestions for parents and educators seeking to help foster intellectual character in themselves and in those under their care. While I am going to speak primarily to educators in this section, most of these suggestions, with a few small tweaks, are equally applicable to the critically important teaching that takes place in the home.

Principle 1: "Begin with the End in Mind"

Having a clear understanding of what it is you want to achieve is critical to the success of any significant undertaking. Without this vision, well-intentioned action is often impotent, if not counterproductive. As Stephen Covey wrote in his best-selling book, *The Seven Habits of Highly Effective People,* "An effective goal . . . identifies where you want to be, and, in the process, helps you determine where you are. It gives you important information on how to get there, and tells you when you have arrived. It unifies your efforts and energy. It gives meaning and purpose to all you do. And it can finally translate itself into daily activities."[1] This is especially true when it comes to the development of intellectual character, where the aim will initially be novel to many of the teachers and administrators called on to implement it.

Therefore, in order for a curriculum of intellectual character development to be successful, we need to begin by ensuring that the entire faculty has a clear understanding of the goal—that is, they must understand what intellectual character is and why it is important. Perhaps the best way to accomplish this is to assign some summer reading on the topic for both the faculty and the administration. The reading can then act as the basis of discussions during the weeks leading up to the new school year and during teacher in-service days throughout the implementation of the program. This book could fill that need, but there are a number of other books listed in the appendixes that could be used as well.

When the goal is understood and valued, the real work begins. A comprehensive reassessment of a school's curriculum in light of intellectual character is the next important step. Because this step includes the potential for a tremendous amount of work, even teachers who appreciate the importance of intellectual character may be initially resistant. Matters are not helped by the fact that many good teachers are justifiably cynical about the multitude of new programs that their administrators regularly introduce as the latest cure to the ills of modern education. These new educational fads often promise the world but almost always produce little by way of positive change and much in the way of added paperwork and bureaucratic headaches. In other words, not only must teachers be convinced that intellectual character really matters, but the process of implementation must be done in a way that limits cynicism by minimizing disruptions to the classroom. As a result, the best idea is often to utilize patterns already in place.

At Rosslyn Academy the greatest opportunity for bringing meaningful change to the school culture comes every five to seven years as the school gears up for its accreditation visits. In the most recent accreditation cycle, Rosslyn decided to take advantage of this enforced period of reflection to begin integrating the language and principles of intellectual character into the curriculum. The school began by reconsidering the type of person it was trying to produce (appendix A). The committee responsible for crafting the school's ultimate aims agreed that intellectual character should not just act as a cosmetic complement to the school's content- and skill-related goals but instead should be at the very heart of its program. Believing that intellectual character and virtuous thinking habits were at the core of "a life transformed by a personal relationship with Jesus Christ," the school made an explicit commitment to analyze its "current programs and curricula to align" itself to the "new student objective" of character development.[2] By making intellectual character a central and driving aim of the

school (and an aim that they would be judged by in the next accreditation cycle), Rosslyn was taking an important step toward
seeing intellectual character development successfully implemented in its curriculum. They had begun "with the end in mind."[3]

PRINCIPLE 2: THE PROVERBS 22:6 PRINCIPLE, "START CHILDREN OFF ON THE WAY THEY SHOULD GO"

While the implementation of this new vision is in its initial stages,
one strategy for teaching intellectual character has already been
tested in Rosslyn's elementary school. This strategy serves to highlight a second principal key to the successful integration of intellectual character in the curriculum—that is, starting early. Like any
type of character development, the foundations of good thinking
habits are created during our first years. While it is never too late
to begin a pursuit of intellectual virtue, our character is most mal-
leable when we are young; therefore, we give our children a wonderful head start when we consciously work to teach virtuous
thinking at an early age.

Because Rosslyn's curriculum already called for morning devotionals, a few teachers decided to create a series of devotionals centered on teaching a different intellectual virtue at each grade level.
The devotional series (of which more details are found in appendix
B) included the reading of at least one story illustrating the intellectual virtue being taught, a series of questions chosen to bring
out the intellectual virtue on display in the story, a children's song
that reinforced the virtue, the memorization of a Bible verse high-
lighting the virtue, and a popular children's video on the virtue.
Significantly, during the one to two weeks that each devotional
program was piloted, the teachers looked for ways in which the
message of the devotionals could be explicitly applied to the academic work of their students. For instance, if a challenging new
math concept was being taught, the teachers would have the class

recite their memory verse on perseverance, sing the song about tenacity or remind the students of the heroic example of intellectual tenacity found in the story they had read together. By applying the devotional to the daily academic challenges of their young students, these teachers were effectively nurturing intellectually virtuous habits.

PRINCIPLE 3: THE TEFILLIN PRINCIPLE (DEUTERONOMY 6:8)

The choice made by these elementary teachers to keep the concepts and principles of intellectual character at the front of these children's minds highlights a third important principle of integration that I am calling the tefillin principle. Directly after the presentation of the Ten Commandments in Deuteronomy 5, Moses tells Israel, "These commandments that I give you today are to be upon your hearts. Impress them on your children. Talk about them when you sit at home and when you walk along the road, when you lie down and when you get up. Tie them as symbols on your hands and bind them on your foreheads. Write them on the doorframes of your houses and on your gates" (Deuteronomy 6:6-9).

Orthodox Jews for centuries have taken this message to heart and have created boxes that can be strapped to a person's arms or forehead that include within them portions of Scripture. These boxes are called tefillin and stand as a powerful illustration of the importance of keeping the vision of intellectual character front and center in our schools. One thing that Rosslyn has done to accomplish this aim has been the placement outside each high school classroom of wooden plaques with one of the intellectual character traits beautifully engraved into it. Each teacher has chosen the intellectual character trait that he or she believes is most relevant to the challenges of the subject matter taught in that room and has made a commitment to integrating the pursuit of that virtue within the curriculum. The plaques serve a number of important purposes. They stand as reminders to both the students and their teachers of their common pursuit of truth. Because the plaques are so visible, they also act as a source of accountability to the community at Rosslyn, reminding students and faculty alike that they are called to a higher standard of learning—one that puts truth and understanding above expedience and the report card. And finally, because the plaques use the same terminology, they act to create a common language from which intellectual character can be understood and discussed.

Principle 4: You've Got to Talk the Talk

As we have just seen, the plaques that Rosslyn has placed outside its classrooms keep the concept of intellectual character before the community, but they also help create a common vocabulary that is becoming an important part of the school's culture. This common language is no small thing. Consider the following conversation between two biochemists.

Biochemist Bob: "The signaling results look interesting, Bernadette, but what was your MAPK assay?"

Biochemist Bernadette: "Well, Bob, it was actually pretty straightforward. Anti-phospho-specific antibodies were used to detect MAPK activity in Swiss 3T3 fibroblasts."

Biochemist Bob: "Yeah, I suppose a kinase assay would have been a bit tricky."[4]

While Bob and Bernadette's conversation does exclude those who do not understand their language—that is, 99 percent of the world's population—this little exchange nevertheless illustrates several important benefits that result from a community sharing a common set of terms.

A common language makes it easier to talk and think efficiently and precisely about something. When, for instance, everyone understands the terms and concepts of intellectual character, you don't have to have a twenty-minute discussion about the meaning and purpose of each term every time it is used. In addition, because everyone understands the term already, you can skip over the basics and move on to meaningful and fruitful interaction with the concept. Imagine if biochemists like Bob and Bernadette had to sit down and define each term that they used each time they used it. Their ability to conduct research would be sabotaged from day one. Not only would large amounts of time be wasted, but the foundation of understanding that the common vocabulary provides would disappear—and with it would go any real chance of new and useful insights in the field. In the same way, when schools take on the language of intellectual character, they make it much more likely that the concepts will sink in and produce fruit.

There is one additional benefit of adopting the vocabulary of intellectual character. Based on the Sapir-Whorf hypothesis, which argues that our intellectual horizons are largely limited by the potential of our vocabulary, it can be argued that our ability to understand, and therefore internalize, the concepts and values of intellectual character will be stilted unless we use a vocabulary equal to the purpose.[5] The phrase *intellectual character* is an excellent example of this point. To me, the importance of intellectual character is now as obvious as gravity. And yet, it was not until philosopher Jason Baehr told me about his work on the subject that I even began to take notice of its existence, let alone see the profound influence it has on our lives.[6] In short, the vocabulary Jason provided gave me eyes to see. I believe the same will be true for your children both at home and in the classroom.

PRINCIPLE 5: TEACHING AND MODELING
EFFECTIVE THINKING ROUTINES

One of the most practical ways to encourage the development of intellectual character is the teaching and modeling of strategic thinking routines. Simple and easy to use, these thinking routines act as an important bridge connecting our day-to-day thinking with our intellectually virtuous aims. For instance, while we may see it as a tool limited to science, the scientific method (the simple process of creating a hypothesis, using evidence to test that hypothesis and then revising the original hypothesis based on the evidence) is one thinking routine that can have a dramatic influence on our ability to quickly and efficiently get to the truth. In fact, it was largely the application of this thinking strategy that produced the unprecedented explosion of scientific knowledge in Europe and the birth of the modern world.[7]

The well-known practice of creating pro-and-con lists is another deceptively simple thinking routine that, if internalized and used regularly, can significantly improve our ability to get and use truth. Many of our decisions are driven by emotion, and often subconscious emotion at that. The act of regularly taking a minute to write down the advantages and disadvantages of a particular choice can, therefore, help ensure that our decision making is not always determined by the capricious power of our emotions. Just as important, by giving us trustworthy reasons for being excited or concerned about a particular choice, thinking routines like the pro-and-con list can turn reason and emotion from being adversaries into being allies. In other words, in addition to consistently producing better decisions, by helping to get our minds and our hearts on the same page, thinking routines play a fundamental role in producing a healthy and well-adjusted life.[8]

Although many of us regularly create pro-and-con lists, the process often stops prematurely. For while we may produce a list, we usually fail to acknowledge the obvious fact that not all the items on the list are equally important. For example, when buying a house, the color of the countertops, the number of bedrooms and the quality of the neighborhood may all be on our list, but they are not all of equal significance. Unless we regularly prioritize our lists, this important thinking routine will lose much of its potency.

Another thinking routine that is particularly useful when assessing the tidal wave of opinions we are confronted with daily is an adaptation of the scientific method called CSQ. This thinking routine was developed in schools as a way to encourage critical thinking, but if internalized it can be used effectively in all walks of life. CSQ is short for three questions that can help us evaluate the legitimacy of any sort of truth claim: (1) What is the *claim*? (2) What is the *support*? (3) What reasons do I have to *question* the evidence (and/or) the claim?[9] Let me give one illustration from the world of politics.

A relatively consistent claim you hear in today's political climate is that the American mainstream media have a liberal bias. Because the mainstream media continue to possess considerable influence on our political process, this is a significant claim. As someone who wants to be fair-minded and careful in my thinking, I do not want to simply accept a serious accusation like this (and I certainly don't want to pass it on) without having investigated whether the claim is true. In other words, I want to know the truth, but I need a thinking routine like CSQ to help me get there. Beyond the obvious benefits of seeking evidence that this routine includes, CSQ also adds an important third component that requires us to evaluate the legitimacy or the biases of our sources. Of course, just because someone has a bias (and we all do) does not mean they are not correct. It only means that we need to be cautious when evaluating the evidence that person presents. For instance, claims by the mainstream media that they are completely objective should be treated as cautiously as claims of mainstream media bias by the "new media." In the end we need reliable evidence if we are to be justified in supporting or rejecting any truth claim, and thinking routines help us identify this evidence efficiently.

A third helpful thinking routine, KWL (Know—Want to know—Learned), has also come out of the world of education.[10] Its primary value is in helping us harness the knowledge base we already have while bringing our attention to those pieces of information that are still required in order to solve the problem. While this is common sense, many of us are hampered in our pursuit of understanding because we are not even clear on what it is we need to know. As Donald Rumsfeld famously noted, "There are known knowns . . . there are known unknowns. . . . But there are also unknown unknowns—the ones we don't know we don't know."[11] KWL forces us to consider what we do and do not know and, in the process, opens up new avenues for investigation and creative solutions to old problems.

Beyond their value in helping us get to the truth more effectively, there is one final, and extremely important, function served by the thinking routines we have surveyed in this chapter. They force us to engage in thinking about our thinking, something that psychologists call metacognition. This habit of critically reflecting on our own thinking is an essential ingredient in our ability to improve the efficiency of our minds.[12] Metacognitive people are concerned not just with what they need to know but with what thinking strategies are best suited to achieve that end. Like the enterprising manufacturing engineer who is always looking for a way to make the production process more efficient, by taking the time to critically reflect on their thinking process, metacognitive people ensure that they will be increasingly good stewards of their intellectual gifts.

Thinking routines are simple, easy to use, and often common

sense. However, that does not mean they will naturally be internalized. On the other hand, it also does not mean that they should be taught in the abstract like some algebraic equation. Instead, to be effectively internalized, thinking routines need to be taught in the context of the pursuit of truth. For instance, when introduced as a means of tackling a controversial or interesting question posed by a teacher or parent, these routines suddenly are seen for what they are—powerful tools for helping us efficiently get to the truth.

Principle 6: Don't Be Afraid of a Few Carrots

None of us are as intellectually virtuous as we would like to be. We are not always, or perhaps even often, driven by an unblemished love of truth. As a result, there are times when our pursuit of intellectual character can benefit from external encouragement. Students are no different. While the aim of intellectual character development is a person who is driven by a love of truth, you will search in vain for a student who always places truth above expediency. Therefore, any path to the successful development of intellectual character needs to be rooted in a sober assessment of students' attitudes and motivations.

As any teacher will tell you, if you want students to pay special attention to something, let them know that they will be tested on it. This principle also applies to the development of intellectual character. Of course, it is difficult to grade character. You can't really quantify it. And for individual acts, you can't always know whether an isolated act genuinely reflects the inner intellectual character of that person. Nevertheless, over time, we do come to know a tree by its fruits. It is in this general sense that you can—and should—hold students accountable for the development of their intellectual character. One way you can do this is by including in a school's assessment plan explicit references to a student's intellectual character. Initially at least, assessing intellectual character will increase student interest in intellectual character more than any appeal to its inherent value. Assessment is also a powerful statement to both the students and their parents that intellectual character is important to the school. Finally, assessment is another way to keep the language and ideas of intellectual character development front and center for the faculty, serving to remind them of the ultimate purpose of their teaching.

The following are three examples of how intellectual character is being assessed in two different schools. While, as we have already seen, it is difficult to assign students a numerical or alphabetical grade for intellectual character, Rosslyn Academy has created a series of teacher comments that can be used in conjunction with the traditional grading scheme. The comments (which are found in appendix C) assess the intellectual character traits that the teacher sees developing behind the grades. Often, good grades follow growing intellectual character, and poor grades result from poor intellectual character. Seeing this connection can be a powerful illustration to both parents and students of the connection between who we are and what we produce. However, there are times when there is a discrepancy between the students' grades and the assessments of their intellectual character. For bright students whose natural ability has become a hindrance to the development of their character, a poor intellectual character assessment can serve to remind them that while all is well in the short term, unless there is a change, the students' promising talents are likely to be squandered. Conversely, for some students whose grades are disappointing, a positive assessment of their intellectual character can act as an encouragement to keep pushing on, and a confirmation that their hard work is admired and valued. In sum, when placed next to students' grades, these comments can simultaneously explain why their grades are what they are and redirect their focus away from grades they get and toward the people they are becoming.

Rosslyn Academy has also recently initiated an award called the Berean Bursary (appendix D). This award is given each year during the graduation ceremony to the student who best exemplifies intellectually virtuous character. Nominated and voted on by the faculty, the Berean Bursary is a dramatic and public statement of the school's values and an encouragement to the students coming up through the ranks to continue their hard work.

The National Honor Society of the Bear Creek School in Redmond, Washington, provides the third example of how intellectual character can be assessed in meaningful and symbolically potent ways. Taking its cue from the National Honor Society's general emphasis on character, the Bear Creek School has chosen to emphasize intellectual character by making it an element of the selection process for potential chapter candidates. As part of their applications students are required to provide an intellectual character evaluation form to at least two of their teachers (appendix E). Once submitted by the teachers, these evaluations are considered by the selection committee alongside the students' grades, their extracurricular involvements and evidence of leadership potential in determining their suitability. Similarly to the Berean Bursary, by making intellectual character a central feature of the National Honor Society, The Bear Creek School is making a statement to its community that the character of their students' minds matters at least as much as the grades they get.

Principle 7: You've Got to Walk the Walk

All the principles we have looked at so far are complementary and work best when they are used together. None of them will be effective alone, and in that sense none of them are indispensible to the project of integrating intellectual character into the school culture. That being said, there is one principle that is as close to being indispensible as you can get. If we are going to be successful in teaching virtuous thinking habits, we need to be living, breathing examples of intellectual character. If you are at all like me, this news, while expected, can still be deflating. For when I honestly look at the character of my own thinking, I see as much vice as virtue. Even when I am involved in a headlong pursuit of knowledge, my motivations are usually mixed. But the reality of our own imperfections does not have to be an impediment to successfully modeling intellectual virtue. The example students need in their teachers is not one of perfection (which, this side of eternity, is always going to be a nonstarter) but rather a model of the *pursuit* of intellectual character. With our words we can establish the ideals, but what they need to see from us is what it looks like to be striving toward those ideals.

So what does that look like? To begin with, it means that we are actively cultivating in ourselves a love of God's truth. Among other things, this will include putting into practice many of the things discussed in the previous chapter. It will also mean consciously applying intellectual character to the *way* we teach. That shouldn't be too tough. After all, many of us went into teaching because we loved the subject matter. Modeling intellectual character (to at least some extent) can be done simply by reminding ourselves why we loved our subject and letting that love pour back into our teaching. This may mean taking the time to interact more deeply with a student's essay and then communicating that interaction in the form of insightful written comments or probing questions. It may mean spending a few more minutes in preparation for class discussions in order to create questions and provide feedback that genuinely stimulate our students. It will certainly mean demanding more from both ourselves and our students. But to the degree that we can recapture our love of the material, this won't feel like work.

We also model the pursuit of intellectual character in *what* we choose to teach. By this I don't mean that we drop math in favor of philosophy or that we need to have classes devoted entirely to intellectual character (although as we shall see that can be effective). Indeed, the whole point of intellectual character is that it is not primarily about what we study but how we study—that is, who we are as thinkers. That said, the teacher who believes that intellectual character development is important will look for ways to explicitly teach the virtues. That may mean beginning each week with a quote of the week that highlights a particular intellectual virtue and then, like the elementary teachers at Rosslyn, consciously reinforcing the message of that quote throughout the week's lessons. (See appendix F for some examples.) Some teachers at Rosslyn have even chosen to devote the first week of the year to intellectual character and the virtues that they think will be needed to succeed in their class. At the Bear Creek School, the senior project is explicitly guided by the pursuit of intellectual character (see appendix G). While this is not essential, some schools might even consider creating a high school elective on the Christian mind, centered on the intellectual virtues. (See appendix H for one such course that has been offered at Rosslyn Academy.)

The suggestions listed in this chapter are good starting points, but they are probably just the tip of the iceberg. One of the most exciting things about being on the ground floor of a new movement is the amount of uncharted territory that remains to be explored. As a result, creative parents and dynamic faculties committed to integrating intellectual character into their homes and schools should treat these suggestions as both a helpful starting point and a launching pad for new ideas and initiatives.

Conclusion

THINKING SHEEPISHLY?

ON A MAGICALLY WHITE CHRISTMAS IN 1981, I was given my first Walkman and a cassette tape—*The Keith Green Collection*. Of the many powerful songs on that tape, the one that stood out to me as an eleven-year-old boy was "The Sheep and the Goats." In this song, Green recounts the New Testament parable of the final judgment in which those who will spend eternity with God (the sheep) are separated from those who will be eternally apart from God (the goats). Keith Green's closing words still ring in my ears, "The only difference between the sheep and the goats, according to Scriptures, is what they did and didn't DO."[1] It was a musical prophet's powerful call for Christians to begin living out the faith they claimed to have. I was inspired then, and I am inspired now. But today I am moved for a slightly different reason.

I have read and reread that passage in Matthew many times since that day and have become convinced that while Keith Green was technically accurate, he missed the central point Jesus was making. My scholarly friends tell me that the point of many parables is wrapped up in a surprise, and the surprise of this story is not who is rewarded and who is punished but how they both respond to the judgment. The sheep and the goats are both genuinely mystified. When God recounts the things they did that earned them their eternal reward, the confused sheep ask, "When did we see you hungry and feed you, or thirsty and give you something to drink?" (Matthew 25:37). The response of the goats is no different, "But when did we see you . . . a stranger or needing clothes or sick or in prison, and did not help you?" (Matthew 25:44). I always found their confusion curious until I figured out that their confusion was the point. It was the surprise.

What separated the sheep and the goats was not just what they *did*, but *who* they had become. The sheep were mystified because they had become the sort of people who *naturally* did the good and loving thing—it was second nature to them. They represent people whose very core has been transformed and whose character has become a reflection of God's heart. The sheep were rewarded with heaven not because they *did* good, but because they *had become* good.

At this point the parable takes another interesting twist that further emphasizes Jesus' concern with our character. In responding to the confusion of the sheep and the goats, God says, "Whatever you did for one of the least of these, . . . you did for me" (Matthew 25:40, 45). Did God say this because he loves the poor more than the rich? No, Scripture is clear that while God has a special concern for the needy, he loves all people equally and immeasurably. So why does God stress actions done to "the least of these"? The German thinker Johann Wolfgang von Goethe is widely held to have said, "You can easily judge the character of a man by how he treats those who can do nothing for him."[2] Could it be that our actions toward the poor, the unattractive and the powerless are a test of who we really are—at our core? I think that is exactly what Jesus is driving at in this parable. The sheep are not only rewarded because they did good deeds, even good deeds done to the neediest. They are rewarded because they had become the type of people from whom good deeds naturally flow—in all circumstances and toward all people. They had become people whose character reflected the character of God.

In the same way, when Jesus commands us to love God with all our minds, he is not primarily concerned with the external results of our thinking. His concern is much more fundamental. He wants us to grow into being a certain type of people—people whose thinking habits have become so good and so deeply ingrained that all our choices, both big and small, reflect his character and the pursuit of his truth. Like the sheep, whose moral character had been so completely transformed that they naturally, almost unconsciously, did the good and loving thing, the call to love God with our minds is first and foremost about the transformation of the character of our minds.

We are not given a choice about whether we will develop intellectual character. Every day we all make hundreds of choices that build momentum toward either good or bad intellectual character. In that sense, intellectual character is simply a given. It is something we all have, and something we are all in the process of developing. However, we do play an important role in determining what kind of character we will develop. It is my hope that this book will encourage in all of us an uncompromising pursuit of truth and a commitment to becoming people of virtuous intellectual character—people whose thinking is consistently characterized by honesty, carefulness, fair-mindedness, healthy curiosity, humility, tenacity and courage.

The quest for intellectual character will not be quick and painless. Nothing worth its salt ever is. It will require the grueling task of replacing our many bad habits with healthy new ones. It will require the work of the Holy Spirit. And, it will require a lifetime's worth of perseverance. But as we are slowly transformed into being people of virtuous intellectual character, the fruits of this internal revolution will naturally pour into every area of our lives.

Philip Brooks once wrote, "Some day, in the years to come, you will be wrestling with the great temptation, or trembling under the great sorrow of your life. But the real struggle is here, now. . . . Now it is being decided whether, in the day of your supreme sorrow or temptation, you shall miserably fail or gloriously conquer."[3]

In other words, it is the multitude of little decisions that will shape our destinies. That is where our thinking habits are formed. And that is where the battle for our intellectual character needs to begin.

A Discussion Guide for
University and Church Groups

Introduction

1. According to the introduction, what are the key components of "intellectual character"? Would you add anything to the definitions laid out in the introduction? If so, what and why?

2. Why is a love for truth so critical to the development of virtuous intellectual character? Are there times that our society places other aims above the truth? If so, what things are prioritized over truth? Discuss specific examples and the consequences to our culture. Are you ever guilty of placing something else above the truth? If so, what?

3. What benefits might come from having "virtuous intellectual character"? How, for instance, could being a consistently honest, fair-minded, courageous, humble and tenacious thinker positively impact your life? Spend a few minutes brainstorming and making as large a list as you can. As you do, consider also Romans 12:2; 1 Timothy 4:16; 2 Timothy 2:2-7, 15; and Titus 1:1. On the other hand, what negative consequences might come from having bad thinking habits such as being a consistently lazy, biased or careless thinker? Create a list of negative consequences resulting from poor thinking habits.

4. From each of the two lists you have just made, pick a top three. What did you list as the three most important consequences in each category? Why? Discuss.

PART ONE: THE SEVEN INTELLECTUAL VIRTUES

CHAPTER 1: INTELLECTUAL COURAGE

Begin by reviewing the definition of intellectual courage below.

Intellectual courage defined: Those who are intellectually courageous earnestly want to know the truth and so consistently take risks in the pursuit of truth. They are willing to reconsider their own beliefs, even if this scares them. But once they have done so, and come to a belief about what is true, they are willing to stick to their guns, even if the majority mocks or threatens them. (Intellectual cowardice is the corresponding vice.)

1. Can you think of any examples in Scripture of intellectual courage? Why were these acts examples of *intellectual* courage—as opposed to moral courage? What were the varying consequences of these acts of intellectual courage, and what lessons can you draw from these consequences?

2. What is the difference between an act of intellectual courage and intellectually courageous character?

3. Make a list of several instances in which you have acted in an intellectually courageous way. Now make a second list of several instances in which you acted in an intellectually cowardly way. Pick one example from each of these lists. What was it that made you act either with courage or cowardice in that moment?

4. On a scale of one to ten, how would you rate yourself regarding intellectually courageous character (one being extremely poor and ten being perfect). Assuming you did not give yourself a ten, where do you think you fall short? Are there any practical steps you can take toward becoming more intellectually courageous? What are they?

5. Read the following passages from the Bible: Daniel 1:10, 2:12, 2:26-28, 3:13-19 and 4:19-27. Summarize the lesson regarding intellectual courage in a sentence and share your summaries with the group. Are there places in your life where you think you will need the intellectual courage of Daniel? What are they? Courage does not mean reck-

lessness. Is there a way that you can act in both a prudent and a courageous way in this situation? How?

CHAPTER 2: INTELLECTUAL CAREFULNESS

Begin by reviewing the definition of intellectual carefulness below.

Intellectual carefulness defined: Those who are intellectually careful earnestly want to know the truth and so consistently make sure not to rush to hasty conclusions based on limited evidence. They are patient and diligent in their thinking, careful that they do not overlook important details. (Intellectual hastiness is the corresponding vice.)

1. Can you think of any examples from history or current popular culture of intellectual hastiness or carelessness? What are they? What were the consequences of those acts of careless thinking?

2. List some instances in which you have acted in an intellectually careful way. Do the same for instances when you have demonstrated careless thinking. What were the results in each case?

3. Are you consistently careful in your thinking? On a scale of one to ten (one being extremely poor and ten being perfect), what rating would you give yourself regarding your level of intellectual carefulness? Why did you give yourself this rating?

4. Consider asking the group if they see any patterns of intellectual carefulness or carelessness in your life. Can they give you an honest rating from one to ten? And, if so, what specific examples of careless or careful thinking led them to give you the rating they did? If this is not appropriate for the group, consider posing these questions to your spouse, or perhaps a close friend.

5. If you have discovered any habits of careless thinking in any area of your life, can you think of any simple ways that you can begin to transform those thinking patterns into ones that exemplify carefulness? If so, what are they? What will you need to do to ensure that you can actually put your intention to change into practice?

6. Read the following passages from the Bible: Romans 10:2, Philippians

1:9-10, 1 Thessalonians 5:21, 1 Timothy 4:16 and Titus 2:7-8. Summarize
in point form the lessons of each passage concerning intellectual carefulness. Discuss your summaries as a group. How can we apply these
lessons to our own lives?

Chapter 3: Intellectual Tenacity

Begin by reviewing the definition of intellectual tenacity below.

Intellectual tenacity defined: Those who are intellectually tenacious earnestly want to know the truth, so they are consistently unwilling to give up
when they find an assignment difficult or boring. Instead, they are determined to fight through the difficulty in order to gain a deeper understanding of the material. (Intellectual laziness is the corresponding vice.)

1. What is it about tenacity in general that we find so inspiring? What
   examples of tenacity (intellectually or otherwise) have been especially
   encouraging to you? Can you think of a specific example of intellectual tenacity from history, Scripture or your own life? Share why
   these examples are particularly inspiring to you.

2. Make a list of the sort of challenges you face in your day-to-day life
   that might require intellectual tenacity. When was the last time that
   you faced a significant challenge in your thinking? How did you respond? What was the result?

3. Some of the obstacles we face in our thinking are not the intimidating
   sort of difficulties that inspire fear so much as they are challenges to
   endure something unpleasant or boring. Why is the challenge to fight
   through boredom so potentially important? Can you think of a personal example of a time in which you faced that sort of challenge?
   How did you respond, and what resulted from your response?

4. From one to ten (one being extremely poor and ten being perfect),
   how would you rate yourself in the area of intellectual tenacity? When
   and where are you most likely to display a lack of intellectual tenacity?
   Can you think of practical ways in which you can begin to alter your
   thinking patterns in an intellectually tenacious direction?

5. Read the following passages from the Bible: Titus 1:9, Hebrews 5:14 and James 1:2-5. Summarize in point form the lessons of each passage concerning intellectual tenacity. Discuss your summaries as a group. How can we apply the lessons in these passages to our lives?

CHAPTER 4: INTELLECTUAL FAIR-MINDEDNESS

Begin by reviewing the definition of intellectual fair-mindedness below.

Intellectual fair-mindedness defined: Those who are intellectually fair-minded earnestly want to know the truth, so they consistently listen in an even-handed way to differing opinions, even if they already have strong views on the subject. In addition, they attempt to view the issue from the perspective of those they disagree with, believing that they do not always have the most complete or accurate vantage point on a given issue. As a former student of mine correctly observed, the intellectually fair-minded person "seeks to know, not to be right." (Intellectual bias is the corresponding vice.)

1. The concept of fair-mindedness is based on a belief in an objective truth. Without the concept of objective truth, there is nothing to be either fair-minded or biased about. But the very concept of objective truth is being questioned in Western culture today. What are the arguments in favor of the relativity of truth? Why do you think these arguments are appealing to many? What are the arguments in favor of the existence of objective truth? (For a concise account of the debate and a powerful argument in favor of truth, see Princeton professor Harry Frankfurt's short but powerful book, *On Truth.*)

2. What are some of the ways in which consistent fair-mindedness can positively affect our lives? And, by way of contrast, what are some of the ways that being consistently biased can negatively affect our lives?

3. Can you think of examples of biased thinking from popular culture? Pick a few of the most important and discuss how these examples affect society.

4. What do you think are the root causes of biased thinking? Based on

your answers, what are some practical ways that we can attack these causes in our own lives in the pursuit of genuine fair-mindedness?

5. Read the following passages from the Bible: Acts 15:1-31 and James 3:17. In point form, summarize the lessons from these passages concerning intellectual fair-mindedness. Discuss your summaries as a group. How can the lessons from these passages be applied to our lives?

Chapter 5: Intellectual Curiosity

Begin by reviewing the definition of intellectual curiosity below.

Intellectual curiosity defined: Those who are intellectually curious earnestly want to know the truth, so they are always asking why. They are not satisfied with the easy and simplistic answers, but have a desire to understand what makes it all work—at the foundational level. For them, learning is not simply a necessary evil (the means of getting a job and buying a house) but a lifelong quest full of mystery and joy. (Intellectual indifference is the corresponding vice.)

1. What are the key differences between the positive and negative types of curiosity? Create a list of various examples of curiosity. Then discuss whether each is an example of virtuous intellectual curiosity, the unhealthy sort of curiosity or could be in either category depending on the circumstances.

2. Create a list of people you know who are shining examples of intellectual curiosity. How does their intellectual curiosity spill over into their everyday lives? And what are the positive fruits that they reap as a result of their habit of intellectual curiosity?

3. Create a list of people you know who are examples of an unhealthy form of intellectual curiosity. What are the negative effects of this sort of curiosity in their lives?

4. Are you consistently intellectually curious? From one to ten (one being extremely poor and ten being perfect), how would you rate your intellectual character in the area of curiosity? Why did you give yourself the score you did?

5. Read the following passages from the Bible: Proverbs 2:1-11 and Acts 17:11, 16-34. In point form, summarize the lessons of these passages concerning intellectual curiosity. Discuss your summaries as a group. How can we apply these lessons to our lives?

Chapter 6: Intellectual Honesty

Begin by reviewing the definition of intellectual honesty below.

Intellectual honesty defined: Those who are intellectually honest want to encourage the spread of truth, so they consistently use information in an unbiased way. Realizing that the strength of any argument lies in the integrity of its evidence and logic, the intellectually honest person is careful not to use information taken out of context, to exaggerate, to distort or to otherwise mislead using statistics or any other type of supporting evidence. In addition, the intellectually honest person does not take credit for evidence or ideas that are not their own; they are careful to cite the work of others whenever it is used. (Intellectual dishonesty is the corresponding vice.)

1. Can you think of examples of intellectual dishonesty in Scripture, in popular culture or in your own life experience? In each of these cases, how did the person or persons apply or communicate truth in a deceptive way? If they were successful in the short term, what are the possible long-term consequences of their intellectual dishonesty—for them and for those touched by their dishonesty? Were the long-term consequences of their intellectual dishonesty different from the short-term consequences? If so, how?

2. Can you think of a public figure (either in Scripture or in current political life) who has maintained a reputation for intellectual honesty and integrity? How has this person earned this reputation?

3. Sadly, we can all point to examples in our own lives of intellectual dishonesty. Make a list of personal examples of intellectual dishonesty. Then go down the list and ask yourself why you chose to be intellectually dishonest in that situation. If you are comfortable sharing, choose one example from your list and share it with the group.

4. In what area of your life are you most tempted to consistently manipulate or fudge the truth? Why do you think the temptation to be
   dishonest is particularly strong in this area of your life? What are
   some consequences that are likely to result from your dishonesty?
   And what are some practical things you can do to begin to develop
   intellectual honesty in this area?

5. Read the following passages from the Bible: 2 Samuel 12:1-14 and
   James 5:19-20. In point form, summarize the lessons of these passages
   concerning intellectual honesty. Discuss your summaries as a group.
   How can these lessons be applied to our lives?

CHAPTER 7: INTELLECTUAL HUMILITY

Begin by reviewing the definition of intellectual humility below.

Intellectual humility defined: Those who are intellectually humble earnestly want to know the truth, so they consistently recognize that they,
like all people, are sinful and capable of error. They are humble because
they are aware that truth is not of their making but is God-breathed. They
are also honest enough to admit the limitations of their own knowledge
base and actually rejoice when they are proved wrong because it means
they have grown in their understanding of God's truth. However, intellectually humble people are also aware that all people are sinful and
limited in knowledge; thus, they are not willing to passively accept the
opinions of others. They remain courageous in their passionate pursuit of
truth even as they admit their own limitations. (Intellectual arrogance is
the corresponding vice.)

1. C. S. Lewis says that "if you think you are not conceited, it means you
   are very conceited indeed" (*Mere Christianity*). Do you think he is
   right? Why or why not?

2. Do you know anyone who you believe has genuinely humble intellectual character? Who is it? What impresses you most about his or
   her life? What does this person do regularly that demonstrates intellectual humility?

3. How can our understanding of human nature (basically good, evil or a mix of the two) influence our quest toward intellectual humility? What do you believe about human nature? Do you apply the same standard to yourself that you apply to others?

4. On a scale of one to ten (one being extremely poor and ten being perfect), how intellectually humble do you think you are? With regard to intellectual humility, what patterns of thought or actions can you point to as examples of good or bad intellectual character?

5. Read Philippians 2:1-11. In a sentence, summarize the point of this passage. Discuss how the lesson of the passage can apply to our thinking.

PART TWO: THE FRUITS OF INTELLECTUAL CHARACTER

CHAPTER 8: THE BENEFITS OF KNOWING MORE ABOUT MORE

1. This chapter claims that ignorance is not usually blissful and that knowledge of the truth almost always produces positive outcomes in our lives. List and discuss some examples from your own life in which ignorance was harmful and knowledge helpful.

2. While knowing the truth is almost always beneficial, are there ever times when knowing the truth is more of a burden than a benefit? What might be some examples in which this seems to be the case? When knowing the truth is painful, does that mean it is ultimately harmful? Discuss.

3. Create a list of five books or people whose insights or knowledge have changed your life for the better. Why did you include the books or people that you did? Share your list with the group and explain how the knowledge you gained from one of the books or one of the people changed your life for the better.

4. In what area of your life do you think you are in the most urgent need of an increase in quality knowledge? Why? What are some practical—and realistic—ways you might go about gaining the knowledge that you feel you need?

CHAPTER 9: THE BENEFITS OF BETTER THINKING

1. Have you ever cut corners in your pursuit of knowledge? When? Why did you do it? What was the result in the short term? How might that choice have affected your intellectual character?

2. Think of an example of when you did not cut corners—when you pushed through and did the hard work necessary to really understand something. What made you work hard in this case but cut corners in the earlier example? What was the result of your hard work in the short term? How might that effort have paid off in the long run?

3. In education circles, the skills of critical thinking and problem solving have gained almost legendary status. They are often viewed as the magic bullets that will turn potential school dropouts into sharp students and model citizens. This book implies that the focus on thinking skills *alone,* while important, is shallow and is unlikely to produce virtuous change in people's lives. Why? Do you agree or disagree?

CHAPTER 10: LOVING GOD

1. Begin by reading the parable of the bags of gold (Matthew 25:14-30) and the parable of the ten minas (Luke 19:12-27). In each of the parables, who was rewarded? Why? Who was punished or condemned? What sort of language was used to describe them? Why do you think they were judged this way?

    Now read Mark 12:30-31. How might this passage be related to the two parables above? If using our God-given talents to the best of our abilities is an act of worship, does that mean that failing to do so is sinful? Why or why not?

2. Read Psalm 136. What kinds of knowledge are critical in worshiping God according to this psalm? Can you think of other psalms, or other passages of the Bible, in which additional types of knowledge are also important to worship? How might attempts to worship without knowledge be dangerous? Emotion is an important part of worship. How might knowledge of the truth aid in our emotional response to God?

3. Read Psalm 19:1-6 and Romans 1:20. What do these passages say about the relationship between our knowledge of the world and our ability to worship God? Some people know a tremendous amount about the world and yet fail to honor the Creator of that world. What might explain this, and what are some passages that would support your explanation?

For the Christian, however, it seems clear that a growing understanding of creation will bring with it an increased ability to honor the Creator. What are some examples in your own life where an increase in knowledge has led to deepening worship?

Chapter 11: Loving Your Neighbor

1. Think back on the examples of the reckless decisions by the businessman and the reporter at the beginning of this chapter. Create a list of harmful effects that their reckless decision making could have had on others. Can you think of examples where hasty, ignorant or otherwise poor decision making by others has resulted in harm to you? Can you think of examples when your own lack of virtuous decision making has caused pain to others?

2. Consider knowledge and trust in the context of intellectual character. Car mechanics generally have a poor reputation. In fact, their reputation is often just slightly better than that of used-car salesmen. Assuming that mechanics are not inherently more deceptive than anyone else, why do you think that we have such a tough time trusting them? Compare how you feel and act around people whom you trust, on the one hand, with how you feel and act around those who have broken your trust, on the other. What good things result from the experience of a trusting relationship or community? What harmful or painful things come out of relationships or communities where trust has broken down?

According to this chapter, and your own thinking, what is the relationship between intellectual character and trust? And, what is the relationship between trust and being able to love your neighbor? Can you think of practical examples from your own life where trust has improved your ability to love others? Can you think of practical examples from your own life where broken trust has hurt your ability to love others?

3. This chapter argued that the acts of intellectual character by Mutava Musyimi and Václav Havel were also acts of love. How so? Can you think of examples from history, Scripture or your own experience where an act of intellectual character has been loving in a similar way?

PART THREE: BECOMING PEOPLE OF INTELLECTUAL CHARACTER

Chapter 12: Developing Virtuous Intellectual Character

1. We have already seen that all of us, at some point, put other things above our loyalty to truth (whether it is our pursuit of wealth, power or popularity, or simply our desire to be loved or accepted). Unfortunately, to the extent that we continue to do this, we are undermining our efforts to develop virtuous intellectual character. Unless we attack the root, we can hack at the leaves forever without seeing any meaningful results. So what can we do to develop a deep love of truth? Using this chapter and your own ideas, create a list of ways that you can effectively grow in your love for truth. For Christians, also consider what role the study of the Bible and the Holy Spirit play in this transformation.

2. We will never seek to become people of increasing intellectual character if we believe we are already intellectually virtuous. Take a minute to recall how you and your friends assessed your intellectual character in each of the different virtues. In what areas do you see the greatest need for growth? Are there thinking habits that are encouraged by your work, your current leisure habits or the people you spend your time with that are harmful to intellectual character? What are they? What steps can you take to replace those habits with new

and positive ones? From your list of bad habits, try picking one habit that you believe can be overcome and create a reasonable plan of attack. Discuss this plan with at least one other person in the group, specifically looking for ways to make it more realistic to implement.

Chapter 13: Seven Suggestions for Educators and Parents

1. By this time, you have likely begun to understand the power of intellectual character to shape the outcome of our lives. You have also seen that our intellectual character must be rooted in a love for truth. And finally you have seen that each of us has areas where our intellectual character is in desperate need of improvement. Now what? What are some practical steps we can take in our quest to help students, children and colleagues become people of virtuous intellectual character? Spend a few minutes considering the suggestions in this chapter, as well as adding suggestions from the group.

2. Take a minute and come up with a list of people who are inspiring examples of how to pass on virtuous intellectual character to others. They can be friends or role models from history or Scripture. Are there ways that you can keep their example before you as you go about your day—and particularly during those periods when you are targeting a specific habit for change?

3. Even when we are consciously working to change a habit, it can take several weeks before we start seeing real change, and months before our new habits have really taken hold. Once that happens the hard work is over, but until then it can be very hard work and may require more strength than we have on our own. Do you have people who are willing to walk with you on this journey? Who are they? How can they keep you accountable in your pursuit of intellectual character?

Appendix A

THE GRADUATE PROFILE FOR ROSSLYN ACADEMY, 2006-2007 AND 2007-2008 SCHOOL YEARS

Rosslyn's holistic educational program is aimed at developing students whose

- honest spiritual lives
- high personal ethics and character
- outstanding knowledge base and thinking habits
- healthy lifestyle and relationships with others
- and visionary service to the world community

reflect a life transformed by a personal relationship with Jesus Christ. A Rosslyn graduate who receives the best of what we have to offer and gives to others his/her very best will develop in the following categories:

SPIRITUAL

- Understand and personalize the Christian faith
- Integrate biblical principles and values into everyday life
- Practice personal disciplines that lead to healthy spiritual growth
- Nurture a life of grace toward others

CHARACTER

- Demonstrate moral character by exhibiting compassion, trustworthiness, determination and integrity

- Demonstrate self-control in attitude and behavior
- Demonstrate dependability and commitment in completing responsibilities
- Exhibit wisdom through well-informed decisions contributing to a healthy and balanced life

INTELLECTUAL

- Demonstrate intellectual character by exhibiting intellectual tenacity, curiosity, courage, honesty, carefulness and humility in the pursuit of excellence
- Demonstrate the ability to think critically, logically and creatively to solve problems
- Exhibit a well-rounded foundation in the academic disciplines and the arts
- Communicate clearly and expressively in writing and speech
- Effectively use media and technology for academic development

SOCIAL

- Have a healthy appreciation of his or her gifts and limitations
- Display strong interpersonal skills
- Demonstrate a commitment to personal growth by seeking, accepting, evaluating and applying feedback
- Value information from diverse viewpoints and cultural perspectives

SERVICE

- Develop a lifestyle of tangible service to others
- Use a Christian-based framework for interacting with the world and life situations
- Serve intelligently, responsibly and sensitively

- Seek opportunities to contribute to society using personal gifts and talents in a Christlike servant manner
- Understand how to work cooperatively

As this is a new foundational document, Rosslyn has begun analyzing current programs and curricula to align ourselves with these goals. In particular, a new student objective for the next accreditation period will focus on spiritual and character development, which is a major focus of the Profile of Graduates.

Appendix B

INTELLECTUAL CHARACTER
ELEMENTARY CURRICULUM

Suggested Devotional Series for Grades
One Through Three—Rosslyn Academy

GRADE ONE—INTELLECTUAL HONESTY

(the importance of telling the truth)
Stories that illustrate intellectual honesty:

- "The Talking Place" (Ann Judson's story as a missionary to Burma in the 1800s) from *Hero Tales,* vol. 1, pp. 47-49

- Any children's story that illustrates the importance of telling the truth

Discussion questions to accompany story: Based on the story that you select, create a short series of discussion questions meant to bring out the importance of telling the truth.

Songs that speak about intellectual honesty:

- "Stretching the Truth Is Telling a Lie" (Music Machine)

- Any children's song that illustrates the importance of telling the truth

Bible verses for memorization on intellectual honesty:

- Proverbs 6:16-19: "There are six things the LORD hates, seven that are detestable to him: haughty eyes, a lying tongue, hands that shed innocent blood, a heart that devises wicked schemes, feet that are quick to rush into evil, a false witness who pours out lies and a person who stirs up conflict in the community."

- Colossians 3:9-10: "Do not lie to each other, since you have taken off your old self with its practices and have put on the new self, which is being renewed in knowledge in the image of its Creator."

Possible videos/DVDs on intellectual honesty:

- Veggie Tales, *Larry and the Fib from Outer Space*
- Veggie Tales, *Larry Boy and the Rumor Weed*

GRADE TWO—INTELLECTUAL COURAGE

(the importance of standing up for what you know to be true)
Stories that illustrate intellectual courage:

- "Here I Stand" (Martin Luther) from *Hero Tales,* vol. 1, pp. 74-76
- Daniel and the Lions' Den (Daniel 6)
- Shadrach, Meshach and Abednego (Daniel 3)
- "The Death of Becket" (martyrdom for one's beliefs) from *The Moral Compass,* pp. 357-60
- "Taking a Beating for Jesus" (Lottie Moon, Missionary to China [1800s] from *Hero Tales,* 3:125-28)
- "The Man with the Ax" (the Small Woman [Gladys Aylward], China [1900s] from *Hero Tales,* vol. 1, pp. 17-20

Discussion questions to accompany story: Based on the story that you select, create a series of questions that will bring out the importance of standing up for what you know to be true.

Songs that speak about intellectual courage:

- "Oh, to Be a Daniel"
- Any other children's song that highlights intellectual courage

Bible verses for memorization on intellectual courage:

- Daniel 3:16-18: "Shadrach, Meshach and Abednego replied to him, 'King Nebuchadnezzar, we do not need to defend ourselves before you in this matter. If we are thrown into the blazing furnace, the God we serve is able to deliver us from it. . . . But even if he does not, we want

you to know, Your Majesty, that we will not serve your gods or worship
the image of gold you have set up.'"

- Daniel 6:10: "Now when Daniel learned that the decree had been published, he went home to his upstairs room where the windows opened
  toward Jerusalem. Three times a day he got down on his knees and
  prayed, giving thanks to his God, just as he had done before."

Possible videos/DVDs on intellectual courage:

- Veggie Tales, *Rack, Shack and Benny*
- Veggie Tales, *Daniel and the Lion's Den*

GRADE THREE—INTELLECTUAL TENACITY

*(the importance of not giving up when you are looking for an answer, even
when it is really hard work)*

   Stories that illustrate intellectual tenacity:

- *The Little Engine That Could* ("I think I can, I think I can . . .")
- "The Thomas Carlyle Story" from Bennett's *The Moral Compass*, pp.
  339-41
- "The Discontented Pig" from *The Moral Compass*, pp. 189-91
- "John Wesley's Last Letter" (the story of William Wilberforce's battle to
  end slavery) from *Hero Tales*, 4:182-84
- "The Impossible Run" (a story about Eric Liddell of *Chariots of Fire*)
  from *Hero Tales*, 2:83-85

Discussion questions to accompany story: Based on the story that you
select, create a series of discussion questions that will bring out the importance of not giving up when you are looking for an answer, even when
it is really hard work.

   Songs that speak about intellectual tenacity:

- "It's So Great to Be a Beaver," *Animals and Other Things*, by R. Krueger,
  1981
- "One Step at a Time," *Psalty Kid's Praise! 5: Psalty's Camping Adventure,*

by Ernie Rettino and Debby Rettino, Studio: Maranatha! for Kids

Bible verses for memorization on intellectual tenacity:

- Titus 1:9: "[An elder] must hold firmly to the trustworthy message as it has been taught, so that he can encourage others by sound doctrine and refute those who oppose it."

- James 1:2-4: "Consider it pure joy, my brothers and sisters, whenever you face trials of many kinds, because you know that the testing of your faith produces perseverance. Let perseverance finish its work so that you may be mature and complete, not lacking anything."

Possible videos/DVDs on intellectual tenacity:

- Veggie Tales, *Ballad of Little Joe*
- Veggie Tales, *Sumo of the Opera*

Appendix C

Assessing Intellectual Character

The following is a list of comments that teachers at Rosslyn Academy are encouraged to use in combination with the student's traditional grade. When placed next to the numerical or alphabetical grade, these comments can serve to explain why the grade is what it is, as well as act as a challenge to students to turn their focus away from the grades and toward the type of people they are becoming.

Examples from Rosslyn Academy's Grade Report Comment List

Teacher comment	The virtue or vice represented
Doesn't give up!	Intellectual tenacity
Gives up too easily	Lack of intellectual tenacity
Thoughtful, probing questions	Intellectual curiosity
Could be more inquisitive	Lack of intellectual curiosity
Not afraid of making mistakes	Intellectual courage
Needs to risk making mistakes	Lack of intellectual courage
Willing to ask questions	Intellectual curiosity and courage
Reluctant to ask questions	Lack of intellectual curiosity and/or courage
Considers other views fairly	Intellectual fair-mindedness and honesty

Won't consider other views	Lack of intellectual fair-mindedness and honesty
Takes the time to do work well	Intellectual carefulness
Regularly careless in studies	Lack of intellectual carefulness
Extremely teachable	Intellectual humility
Difficulty accepting criticism	Lack of intellectual humility
Takes ownership of learning	Intellectual autonomy
Relies on others too much	Lack of intellectual autonomy

Appendix D

THE BEREAN BURSARY

Initiated by Rosslyn Academy, Nairobi, Kenya, during the 2006-2007 academic year.

The following script is used in presenting the Berean Bursary during the graduation ceremony at Rosslyn Academy:

> The Berean Bursary is named after the community of Christians living in Berea, whose passion for the truth served as a model of Christlike intellectual character to the early church. As Acts 17:11 states, "Now the [Bereans] were of more noble character than [the Thessalonians], for they received the message with great eagerness and examined the Scriptures every day to see if what Paul said was true."
>
> The Berean Bursary is given to the graduating senior who best exemplifies the virtuous intellectual character of the Bereans. Each year the high school faculty chooses the one person, from a number of worthy nominees, whose life best reflects a passion for truth as demonstrated in the intellectual character traits of honesty, fair-mindedness, courage, curiosity, carefulness, tenacity and humility. This year it is my pleasure to award the Berean Bursary to _____

Appendix E

THE BEAR CREEK SCHOOL NATIONAL HONOR SOCIETY INTELLECTUAL CHARACTER EVALUATION FORM

Student Name:

Faculty Name:

Date:

THE INTELLECTUAL VIRTUES

At the Bear Creek School our aim is not to turn out students who have merely mastered a certain body of knowledge or have achieved a certain GPA. Instead, we aim to produce students who are earnest seekers of truth and, as a result, have developed fundamental intellectual character traits that will lead them into truth as they go through life—both inside and outside the classroom. Students who gain admission into The Bear Creek School chapter of the National Honor Society should be examples of outstanding intellectual character. Please help us in evaluating this student's intellectual character by reading and filling out the form below.

THE SEVEN INTELLECTUAL VIRTUES DEFINED

Intellectual tenacity: Those who are *intellectually tenacious* earnestly want to know truth, so they are not willing to give up when they find an assignment difficult or boring. They are determined to fight through the difficulty in order to gain a deeper understanding of the material.

In your class, to what degree does this student demonstrate a willingness to press on in the face of a significant intellectual challenge?

(For each of the following categories "0" means "Never" and "10" means "Always.")

0 – 1 – 2 – 3 – 4 – 5 – 6 – 7 – 8 – 9 – 10

Intellectual curiosity: Those who are *intellectually curious* earnestly want to know truth, so they are always asking why. They are not satisfied with the easy and simplistic answers but have a desire to understand what makes it all work—at the foundational level. The intellectually curious person regularly asks questions in class and is an active participant in class discussion.

In your class, to what degree does this student demonstrate a passion for truth?

0 – 1 – 2 – 3 – 4 – 5 – 6 – 7 – 8 – 9 – 10

Intellectual honesty: Those who are *intellectually honest* earnestly want to know truth, so they consider everything in an unbiased way. If they come to an issue with a preconceived view, they don't tune someone else out simply because that person's view contradicts their own. Instead, they listen attentively and reconsider their own views in light of the new information. "They seek to know, not to be right."

In your class, to what degree does this student demonstrate a willingness to put the pursuit of truth above his or her current opinion?

0 – 1 – 2 – 3 – 4 – 5 – 6 – 7 – 8 – 9 – 10

Intellectual courage: Those who are *intellectually courageous* earnestly want to know truth, so they take risks in the pursuit of truth. They are willing to reconsider their own beliefs, even if this scares them. But once they have done so, and come to a belief about what is true, they are willing to stick to their guns, even if the majority mocks or threatens them. The intellectually courageous student is willing to take risks in class assignments in the pursuit of excellence and truth.

In your class, to what degree does this student demonstrate a willingness to risk—either in the pursuit or defense of truth?

0 – 1 – 2 – 3 – 4 – 5 – 6 – 7 – 8 – 9 – 10

Intellectual carefulness: Those who are *intellectually careful* earnestly want to know truth, so they make sure not to rush to hasty conclusions based on limited evidence but instead are patient and diligent, careful that they do not overlook important details. Intellectually careful people check their work on math problems, proofread their essays and are generally concerned about getting it right.

In your class, to what degree does this student demonstrate intellectual carefulness?

0 – 1 – 2 – 3 – 4 – 5 – 6 – 7 – 8 – 9 – 10

Intellectual humility: Those who are *intellectually humble* earnestly want to know truth, so they recognize that they are both sinful and capable of being in error—and finite and thus cannot possibly know all things. As a result, they actually rejoice when they are proved wrong because it means they have grown in their understanding of God's truth. In short, intellectually humble people are subservient to truth, not the other way around. The practical result is that they consistently demonstrate concern for their peers and teachers, treating them with respect and dignity in how they ask questions and in how they accept critiques of their work.

In your class, to what degree does this student demonstrate intellectual humility?

0 – 1 – 2 – 3 – 4 – 5 – 6 – 7 – 8 – 9 – 10

Intellectual autonomy: Those who are *intellectually autonomous* earnestly want to know the truth, so they take full responsibility for their own learning. They are therefore prompt in turning in class assignments, taking tests and getting to class. But more importantly still, while they value the input of teachers and peers, they do not lean on the efforts of these groups to complete their work. Intellectually autonomous people understand that for knowledge to be theirs, they have to be the primary agent in the process.

In your class, to what degree does this student demonstrate intellectual autonomy?

0 – 1 – 2 – 3 – 4 – 5 – 6 – 7 – 8 – 9 – 10

Thank you for taking the time to carefully consider this student's intellectual character.

*Please add up the seven categories and place the total (0-70) at the bottom of the page.

Appendix F

THE BEAR CREEK SCHOOL
SENIOR PROJECT

I. PURPOSE

The purpose of the senior project is to develop intellectual virtue in students by challenging their knowledge base and stretching their faculties as they pursue a meaningful goal that reflects their unique passions, personality and abilities.

Intellectual virtue can be defined as those intellectual character traits found in a person who earnestly wants to know the truth. Examples of intellectual virtue are intellectual curiosity, intellectual tenacity, intellectual carefulness, intellectual courage, intellectual fair-mindedness, intellectual honesty and intellectual humility.

II. CHOOSING A SENIOR PROJECT

The critical component in choosing a senior project is finding something that you are passionate about that fits the project's purpose statement. However, other questions should be considered as well.

- Can the project be completed within the three-and-a-half-week time period?

- Do you have access to the resources needed to complete the project?

- Does the project require you to stretch both your current knowledge base and your imagination? (Will it challenge you?)

- Is the project worth doing? Does it have real value for you or others?

- Does it have measurable objectives?

While the choosing of the project is primarily the responsibility of the student, the student's faculty adviser and the assessment panel must ultimately approve the project. Therefore, it is the responsibility of the students to provide evidence to their faculty advisers and the assessment panel that their proposed project adequately meets the requirements laid out in the project's purpose statement and the questions above. This will be done through a concise written proposal.

III. The Adviser

The choice of a faculty adviser will be made by the assessment panel based on a combination of the following factors: (1) the preference of the student, (2) the compatibility of the project with the expertise of the faculty member and (3) the availability of the faculty member.

IV. Necessary Components and Assessment

Each project will have several required components, including (a) a project journal, (b) a student-created and faculty-approved timetable to which the student must adhere, (c) the completion of a project of high quality, (d) an oral presentation of the project and (e) the oral defense of the project.

(1) Due to the wide diversity of project types, each project will be assessed based on a *rubric* created by the assessment panel. The goal is to move from broad, vague ideas to concretely *measurable objectives.*

(2) The *project timetable* will be created in conjunction with the student's faculty adviser. Meeting the self-imposed deadlines of the timetable will be an important factor in the final assessment of the project.

(3) The *project journal* will include the following things: (a) the project proposal, (b) a timetable for the completion of the project's various components, (c) a half-page summary of each day's project-related work, (d) once-per-week illustrations/photos and (e) a written evaluation of the student's experience with the project. The evaluation should center on what the student felt were the most valuable lessons learned as a result of doing the project, using intellectual virtues as a framework for that discussion.

(4) The project will be presented orally by the student to the assessment panel and to the student's peers. It should be no less than twenty minutes and no more than thirty minutes in length (a warning card will be raised at twenty-eight minutes). The *oral presentation* should address the following points: (a) an explanation of why the student chose the project, (b) an explanation of the project itself, (c) the challenges faced in the process of producing the project, (d) how the student's knowledge base was expanded and (e) what challenges the student faced and how those challenges were overcome. The presentation should be multimedia in nature—ideas include a Power Point, charts or spreadsheets, video, artwork, etc.

(5) The *oral defense* will amount to the answering of questions posed to the presenter by the assessment panel and the audience. The defense will last no longer than fifteen minutes. The presenter will take the first three questions from the assessment panel members and then may take questions from the audience as time allows.

(6) The *evaluation* will be based on all parts of the project, including proposal, meetings with advisers, journal, presentation and defense. The assessment panel will give out final grades before students leave for the senior trip. Possible grades are Honors, Pass or Fail.

* Job shadowing in the field of one's project or the securing of an expert in the field as a mentor is a component that will be required for some but encouraged for all.

V. KEY DATES AND DEADLINES

February 13—Initial project proposals and faculty adviser requests turned in

February 27—Project approval and faculty adviser assignments made

March 1-9—Initial meeting with adviser to clarify project goals

March 10-April 30—Next set of meetings with adviser to construct timetable and discuss project

March 19—Timetable turned in

May 12—Meet with faculty adviser. From now on meet at least one time per week with your faculty adviser.

May 12-14—Senior finals. Early dismissal.

May 14– Project kick-off day (follows last senior final). This is the first group meeting where the seniors will present their project ideas to their classmates and all advisers, answering questions and eliciting feedback.

May 18—The first group meeting will take place on this day during fifth period. The purpose of this meeting will be a chance for each student to present the progress they are making on their project.

May 25—The second group meeting—again, to assess progress—will take place.

June 1—The third group meeting.

June 5-7—Projects should be essentially complete, and a "mock presentation" will be given by each student to his or her faculty adviser and the other student(s) assigned to that adviser.

June 7-9—Presentation of the project. The order of presentations will be decided by drawing names out of a hat on the first day of presentations. Presentations will follow the guidelines described above.

June 12—Graduation! Evaluation of the project mailed to the student.

Appendix G

PHILOSOPHY (THE LOVE OF WISDOM AND TRUTH) AND LOGIC (THE TOOLS NEEDED TO FIND TRUTH)

Rosslyn Academy Course Outline

This class is about something far bigger than a grade or gathering new information. It is about becoming more fully alive. It is my hope that this class will be the beginning of a lifelong passionate pursuit of truth—a pursuit that will deeply enrich your lives and the lives of those around you, and a pursuit that will ultimately lead you into a profoundly personal relationship with the Author of Truth.

I. Why truth matters (1 week)

    A. Essay (10%)

    B. Class discussion (part of the 20% participation grade)

II. What do we need to get to the truth?

    A. Virtuous intellectual character (2 weeks)

        1. What is intellectual character?

        2. Why is it so important?

        3. How do we develop intellectual character?

        4. Personal assessment essay (10%)

        5. Class discussion (part of the 20% participation grade)

    B. A true worldview (2 weeks)

        1. What is a worldview?

    2. What are the main worldviews and how are they similar/different?

    3. Test over worldview learning (10%)

  C. The right intellectual tools—logic (6 weeks)

    1. What is logic and why does it matter?

    2. Introductions and key terms

    3. The categorical syllogism

    4. Other types of syllogisms

    5. Formal fallacies

    6. Informal fallacies

    7. Finding and analyzing logic in popular culture

    8. Major logic exam (20%)

III. The big questions of life and the answers of those who have come before us (3 weeks)

  A. The major schools of philosophy (naturalism/logical positivism, Christian theism, existentialism/postmodernism)

  B. The big questions and the various answers given

  C. The Christian response to life's big questions

  D. Test over the major schools of philosophy (10%)

IV. Applying our training to contemporary culture—the philosophy project (4-5 weeks)

  A. The project description: Each student will have a chance to choose from one of the four general topics below. Having chosen a general topic, the student will have two to three weeks (depending on time constraints and research access) to research and write a six-to-eight-page paper on their topic. Having written the paper, the student will then have twenty minutes to present his or her research to the class. (The paper will act as the final exam [20%], and the presentation will be part of the 20% participation grade.)

  B. The project topics—

    1. Analyze the worldview of a favorite pop star based on his or her

lyrics and discuss at length the implications of that artist's beliefs if lived out authentically.

2. Analyze the worldview and message of three movies (that I have chosen) and discuss at length the implications of these movies' messages if they were authentically lived out.

3. Using logic, analyze the quality of the arguments put forward in at least three major newspaper editorials. What type of argument is it? How is the argument set up? Is that argument formally valid? Are there serious flaws (fallacies) in the thinking (logic) of the author?

4. Discuss the life and ideas of a major philosopher and the possible implications on the lives of people who adhere to these ideas.

Introduction for the
Intellectual Virtues Academy,
Long Beach, California

Charter School Petition
(Under review as of August 2012)

ELEMENT 1: EDUCATIONAL PROGRAM

"A description of the educational program of the school, designed, among other things, to identify those whom the school is attempting to educate, what it means to be an 'educated person' in the 21st century, and how learning best occurs. The goals identified in that program shall include the objective of enabling pupils to become self-motivated, competent, and lifelong learners."

CA Education Code § 47605 (b)(5)(A)

A. Mission and Vision

IVA's *mission* is to create and sustain an atmosphere that inspires significant growth in "intellectual character virtues," which are the deep personal qualities of an excellent thinker, inquirer, or student. Intellectual character virtues include curiosity, wonder, attentiveness, intellectual carefulness, intellectual thoroughness, intellectual autonomy, creativity, open-mindedness, intellectual humility, and intellectual perseverance.

IVA's *vision* is for a small, intellectual virtues–based learning community that is uniquely personal, relational, reflective, active, and academically rigorous. This community will equip all students to think carefully, critically, and creatively. IVA graduates will be on their way to becoming lifelong learners, having productive and successful careers, and living lives of meaning and wisdom.

B. An Intellectual Virtues Educational Model

Given the uniqueness of IVA's educational model, it is important to be clear about what exactly the model involves. In the present section, we provide an overview of an intellectual virtues educational model. We begin by comparing it with several related models.

An intellectual virtues approach to education bears important connections to more familiar and well-established educational approaches. The notions of "character development" and "character education," for instance, have a long and distinguished history (Lickona 1992 and 1993). IVA will incorporate many of the "best practices" of this tradition (these practices are nicely summarized in Lickona and Davidson 2005 and Berkowitz and Bier 2006). There are, however, important differences between traditional approaches to character education and an intellectual virtues approach. The most notable difference is that traditional approaches tend to focus on fostering *moral* or *civic* virtues rather than *intellectual* virtues. Moral virtues are the character traits of a "good neighbor." They include qualities like kindness, compassion, and generosity. Civic virtues are the character traits of a good citizen. They include qualities like integrity, respect, and tolerance. Intellectual virtues, however, are the character traits of a good *thinker* or *reasoner*. Like moral and civic virtues, they involve various beliefs, attitudes, emotions, and abilities. What makes them unique is that they aim at distinctively "cognitive" ends or goals: for example, at the acquisition, understanding, and application of important knowledge. Accordingly, on traditional models of character education, the primary question for teachers and administrators is: "How can we shape and mold the character of our students so that they become good neighbors or citizens?" On an intellectual virtues model, the question is: "How can we shape and mold the character of our students so that they become good thinkers or learners?"

An intellectual virtues approach also has some affinity with educational approaches that focus on the development of certain intellectual *skills*. For instance, several educational theorists have stressed the importance of "metacognition" or "metacognitive strategies" in classroom learning (Waters and Schneider 2010; Ablard and Lipschultz 1998; Coutinho 2008; Deemer 2004; Sperling, Howard, Staley, and Dubois 2004; Yun Dai and Sternberg 2004). This approach is aimed at equipping students with specific strategies or techniques, tailored to their individual learning styles and abilities, that can be actively deployed in the learning process (e.g., semantic webs, concept charts, mnemonics, mind-mapping). Metacognitive strategies have an important place within an intellectual virtues educational model. Like a metacognitive approach, an intellectual virtues approach involves an intentional, active, and intelligent method of learning—one that discourages passive, unreflective, and uncritical reception of information (Winne 1995). But an intellectual virtues approach also has a deeper aim: it seeks to impact students at a basic motivational level, helping them to *value* knowledge, *delight* in learning, and *care* about their intellectual development and growth (Scheffler 1991; Wolk 2008; Goldie 2012).

An intellectual virtues educational model also bears a resemblance to a *critical thinking* model (Sternberg 1986; Siegel 1980, 1988; Ennis 1993). Indeed, intellectual virtues are, as it were, the "flesh and bones" of critical thinking. To be a critical thinker, one must be curious and reflective, and one's thinking must be marked by rigor, carefulness, and fair-mindedness. Thus an intellectual virtues approach is consistent with but also adds important content to a critical thinking approach. It also addresses student *motivation* in a way that a critical thinking approach might not, insofar as a student might know *how* to think critically, but be too dogmatic, stubborn, lazy, or otherwise unmotivated to do so.

As this initial comparison suggests, an intellectual virtues approach has many important benefits:

- It *avoids controversial notions of values and morality* that often accompany more traditional approaches to character education and complicate their integration into educational settings that are increasingly diverse and multicultural. To "buy into" an intellectual virtues approach, one need only accept the value of knowledge, learning, and the personal qualities that facilitate these important goals.

- By targeting student motivation as well as ability, an intellectual virtues approach *bridges the "action-ability gap."* As Harvard education researcher Ron Ritchhart has noted, intellectual virtues—or "thinking dispositions"—"act as both a descriptive and an explanatory construct, making clear the mystery of how raw ability is transformed into meaningful action" (Ritchhart 2002: 34). In other words, in addition to providing students with certain knowledge and skills, an intellectual virtues approach also provides them with drive and desire to deepen and use these important goods.

- By making students careful, critical thinkers, this approach *equips students to cope with and process the barrage of information* that we are all confronted with on a daily basis. Via the internet, television, and other media, we face a steady and potentially overwhelming flow of information. Today more than ever, it is crucial that all citizens be capable of discriminating between true and false, credible and non-credible sources of information. This important capacity consists precisely in the range of intellectual habits and skills fostered by an intellectual virtues approach to education. This approach teaches students to ask the right questions, to demand and evaluate evidence, and to persevere in their pursuit of the facts.

- An intellectual virtues approach *equips students for success in the workplace.* Whether one is a school teacher, paramedic, salesperson, electrician, attorney, artist, or accountant, success at work requires the ability to *think*—to think carefully, critically, and creatively. By promoting the acquisition of important knowledge and the personal qualities that aim at such knowledge, an intellectual virtues approach provides students with many of the "soft skills" that research indicates is vital to career advancement and success in today's economy (Schulz 2008; Andrews and Higgson 2008; www.dol.gov/odep/pubs/fact/softskills.htm).

- An intellectual virtues approach also *prepares students for success beyond the workplace*. As any adult knows, life is filled with difficult challenges, decisions, and questions. Negotiating these aspects of life well requires that one be a careful, thoughtful, reflective thinker; it requires a kind of "wisdom" characteristic of an intellectually virtuous person. In this respect, an intellectual virtues educational model teaches students, not just to learn well, but also to *live* well.

At IVA, we will give special attention to nine "Master Virtues," which are curiosity, intellectual humility, intellectual autonomy, attentiveness, intellectual carefulness, intellectual thoroughness, open-mindedness, intellectual courage, and intellectual perseverance. These virtues fall into three categories, corresponding to three stages or dimensions of learning: getting the learning process started and headed in the right direction; making this process go well; and overcoming challenges to productive learning:

Getting Started

Curiosity: wonders, ponders, asks why; involves a thirst for understanding.

Intellectual humility: an awareness of one's own intellectual limits; a lack of concern with intellectual superiority and status.

Intellectual autonomy: a capacity for active, self-directed thinking; an ability to think and reason; also involves knowing when to trust and rely on others in an intellectual context.

Executing Well

Attentiveness: keeps one focused and on task; zeroes in on important details and nuances of appearance, meaning, etc.

Intellectual carefulness: an awareness of and sensitivity to the requirements of good thinking and learning; quick to note and avoid pitfalls and mistakes.

Intellectual thoroughness: seeks and provides deeper meaning and explanations; not content with appearances or easy answers.

Handling Challenges

Open-mindedness: an ability to "think outside the box"; gives a fair and honest hearing "to the other side"; can also involve an ability to think in creative or original ways.

Intellectual courage: persists in thinking, inquiring, discussion, and other intellectual activities despite the presence of some threat or fear, including fear of embarrassment or failure.

Intellectual perseverance: hangs tight when learning becomes difficult or challenging; keeps its "eyes on the prize" and doesn't give up.

C. An Intellectual Virtues Model in Practice

To provide an even more concrete idea of what an intellectual virtues approach to education will look like at IVA, we identify the following five "signature features" of an IVA education, followed by fifteen well-established methods for fostering intellectual virtues in an educational setting.

Five Signature Features of an IVA Education:

1. *Personal.* IVA's mission is to nurture the deep personal qualities essential to being an excellent and lifelong learner. It is therefore part of the "curapersonalis" or "education of the whole person" tradition in education (Richards 1980; Huebner 1995; Kirby et al 2006). IVA's small size and small classes will ensure that the school is an intimate, friendly, and personal environment. IVA teachers will attend to and nurture the well-being of each student.

2. *Relational.* Character growth occurs most often in the context of relationships. This is a context in which intellectual virtues can be modeled, trust can be built, care can be expressed, and where admiration and emulation are a natural result. IVA teachers will know their students and will actively seek to address their needs. Students will work together in mutually edifying and supportive relationships.

3. *Rigorous.* Intellectual virtues do not arise in a vacuum; rather, they are the product of rigorous and reflective engagement with curricular content. Intellectual virtues aim at a deep understanding and appreciation of important knowledge. For this reason, an intellectual virtues approach to education is not an *alternative* to a rich, standards-based approach. At IVA, the curriculum will be closely aligned with California state standards, and teachers will nurture and inspire a rigorous command of this material.

4. *Reflective.* Growth in the intellectual virtues must be pursued in a reflective, intentional manner. Therefore, students and teachers at IVA will be aware of and attentive to their own intellectual strengths and weaknesses and will use this knowledge to their advantage in the learning process. Students will also be reflective in their engagement with academic content: their teachers will routinely reflect with them on why they are learning what they are learning; and they will be challenged to "think outside the box," generate new ideas and solutions, and consider alternative possibilities.

5. *Active.* Students do not become excellent thinkers or inquirers by being passive recipients of tidily packaged bits of information. Accordingly, students at IVA will be expected to take control of their intellectual growth and development. They will be trained to actively engage ideas, ask good questions, demand evidence, and support and defend their convictions.

Education researchers have identified a range of methods and strategies that, when properly employed, are effective at promoting intellectual and other forms of character development. Of particular significance is recent research on "character education" (Lickona and Davidson 2005; Berkowitz and Bier 2007) and "thinking dispositions" (Ritchhart 2001, 2002; Perkins et al 2000; Tishman, Perkins, and Jay 2009). We briefly enumerate 15 of these strategies below. The role that these strategies will play in IVA's instructional program is clarified later on in Element 1.

Fifteen Research-Based Strategies for Fostering Intellectual Character Virtues:

1. *Creating a "culture of thinking."* A "culture of thinking" is a community in which individual and collective thinking is valued and promoted as part of the regular, day-to-day experience of each member of the community (Ritchhart, Church, and Morrison 2011: 219; Ritchhart 2002; Tishman, Perkins, and Jay 1995). Because excellent thinking is the activity most characteristic of intellectual virtues, cultures of thinking are places in which intellectual virtues are practiced. They involve providing ample time and opportunities for thinking, the use of "thinking routines," attention to "big ideas," and a focus on authentic learning over "working" (Ritchhart 2002).

2. *Staff hiring and development.* An intellectual virtues educational model must be implemented and supported by teachers and administrators who genuinely understand, are passionate about, and are appropriately trained in this model (Berkowitz and Bier 2006; Lickona and Davidson 2005). Schools must give substantial and very careful attention to this fact both in the hiring process and in how they train and support their teachers.

3. *Direct instruction.* Research suggests that direct instruction in intellectual virtues is critical to creating the kind of understanding and climate that nurtures these qualities (Lickona 1993; Lickona and Davidson 2005). This includes instruction in what intellectual virtues are, the different groups or types of intellectual virtues, how intellectual virtues compare with related moral, civic, and cognitive abilities, their role in learning and education, and their importance to living a thoughtful and meaningful life.

4. *Family support.* A culture conducive to intellectual character growth also requires strong family support and involvement (Berkowitz and Bier 2004; Lickona and Davidson 2005). This means that schools must also instruct parents in an intellectual virtues model and must provide them with concrete guidance and opportunities (e.g. through newsletters, online resources, and volun-

teering opportunities) to foster intellectual virtues in their children.

5. *Advisory groups.* Advisory groups allow for ongoing positive relationships between students and intellectual mentors or advisers. They provide a safe environment in which teachers can nurture students' character development through conversation, goal-setting, structured reflection, personal encouragement, and other means (Berkowitz and Bier 2004, 2006).

6. *Ongoing self-reflection and self-assessment.* Self-knowledge is a critical starting point for all manner of personal growth, including intellectual character growth. For this reason, a key feature of an intellectual virtues educational model is ongoing self-reflection and self-assessment, through which students acquire an honest and in-depth understanding of their respective intellectual character strengths and weaknesses (Lickona 1993; Berkowitz and Bier 2007).

7. *Modeling.* Modeling of intellectual virtues by teachers and other school leaders provides students with informative and attractive examples of these traits. These examples evoke admiration and inspiration on the part of students, which in turn lead to their *imitation* of the relevant "exemplars." Research indicates that natural and systematic modeling of intellectual virtues is a powerful means of promoting positive character growth (Caar 2007; Lickona and Davidson 2005; Berkowitz and Bier 2006; Davidson, Khmelkov, and Lickona 2010).

8. *Positive reinforcement.* Calling positive attention to student activity that embodies intellectual virtues is a powerful tool for encouraging such activity and causing it to become "second nature" (Ritchhart 2002; Davidson, Khmelkov, and Lickona 2010). Positive reinforcement of intellectual virtues should occur at multiple levels, for example, through annual awards to students who best exemplify certain key virtues, mid-instruction recognition and praise of student comments or actions, and specific teacher feedback on student work and performance.

9. *Reflective teaching and learning.* Teachers concerned with fostering intellectual character virtues will approach their craft and subject

matter in a thoughtful and reflective manner. They will not be preoccupied with "teaching to the test." Instead, they will model—and thereby promote—*curiosity* and intellectual *passion*, asking challenging and fundamental questions, and regularly identifying what is most interesting and important in what students are learning (Langer 1993, 2000; Rodgers 2002; Kitchener 1983; Baron 1981).

10. *Thinking routines.* Thinking routines are simple cognitive patterns or structures that "consist of a few steps, are easy to teach and learn, are easily supported, and get used repeatedly" (Ritchhart, Palmer, Church, and Tishman 2006; Ritchhart, Church, Morrison 2011; Ritchhart 2002). They include routines for introducing and exploring ideas (e.g. "Think-Puzzle-Explore"), routines for synthesizing and organizing ideas (e.g. "The Micro Lab Protocol" and "Connect-Extend-Challenge"), and routines for digging deeper into ideas (e.g. "Claim-Support-Question") (Ritchhart, Church, and Morrison 2011). (See www.pzweb.harvard.edu/vt/ for more on this topic.) Because such thinking is the basis of many intellectual virtues, thinking routines provide students with wide-ranging opportunities to *practice* and thereby to further develop these traits.

11. *Making thinking visible.* Emerging from the "Visible Thinking" project at Harvard University (www.pzweb.harvard.edu/vt/), "making thinking visible" is a pedagogical approach that involves providing students with explicit representations of the structure and patterns of excellent thinking in order to deepen their content learning and foster critical thinking skills and dispositions (Ritchhart and Perkins 2008; Ritchhart, Church, and Morrison 2011; Tishman and Palmer 2005). This approach fosters intellectual character growth by making explicit, concrete, and visible (e.g. through argument maps, reflective prompts, documentation of students' answers to questions, the use of thinking routines) the specific sorts of thinking, reflecting, and reasoning that are proper to intellectual virtues. It also provides a framework for imitating and practicing these activities.

12. *Metacognition.* "Self-regulating" or "metacognitive" strategies are tech-

niques that can be used to help learners understand, control, and manipulate their cognitive processes (e.g. Cornoldi 2010; Waters and Schneider 2010; Lucangeli 1998; and Winne 1995). They include such strategies as semantic webs, concept charts, mnemonics, and mind-mapping. Metacognitive strategies can be used by teachers to facilitate an active engagement with curricular content on the part of their students. Such engagement sets the stage for and is a crucial step in the formation of "thinking dispositions" or intellectual virtues (Ritchhart 2002).

13. *Critical thinking pedagogy.* "Critical thinking" refers to the "intellectually disciplined process of actively and skillfully conceptualizing, applying, analyzing, synthesizing, and/or evaluating information gathered from . . . observation, experience, reflection, reasoning, or communication" (Scriven and Paul 1987). Research indicates that pedagogical strategies aimed at critical thinking (e.g. case studies, discussion methods, questioning techniques, debates) can enhance academic performance across multiple domains (Paul 2004; Norris 1985; Angelo 1995; Ennis 1993). Because intellectual virtues are the personal foundation of critical thinking (Siegel 1988), critical thinking pedagogy can also be used to foster growth in these traits.

14. *Agenda of understanding.* Intellectual virtues aim at deep understanding of important subject matters (Zagzebski 1996; Roberts and Wood, 2007; Baehr, 2011a). Therefore, teachers can promote intellectual character growth by implementing an "agenda of understanding," which involves "pushing students' thinking and putting students in situations where they have to confront their own and others' ideas" (Ritchhart 2002: 223; Vygotsky 1978; Ritchhart, Church, and Morrison 2011). This approach "stresses exploring a topic from many angles, building connections, challenging long-held assumptions, looking for applications, and producing what is for the learner a novel outcome" (Ritchhart 2002: 222; Wiggins and McTighe 2005).

15. *Incorporating virtue concepts into standards and assessment.* A final but essential way of fostering intellectual virtues is the integration of intellectual virtue concepts into formal assessment. This can be done

in a variety of ways, including the systematic use of virtue-language in standard grading rubrics (e.g. assessing student answers in terms of their *carefulness, thoroughness, creativity,* or *rigor*), the use of "intellectual character portfolios" (Ritchhart, Church, and Morrison 2011), and the assessment of student performance in terms of the *goals* proper to intellectual virtue (e.g. deep understanding or the creative application of knowledge).

D. WHOM IS IVA ATTEMPTING TO EDUCATE?

IVA proposes to serve 150 students in grades 6-8. The school anticipates opening with two sixth-grade classes of 50 students in year one, adding one grade and fifty students per year through year three. Projected enrollment in the first five years is as follows:

Table H.1

	AY 2013-14	AY 2014-15	AY 2015-16	AY 2016-17	AY 2017-18
Grade 6	50	50	50	50	50
Grade 7		50	50	50	50
Grade 8			50	50	50
Total Students	50	100	150	150	150

Educational interests.
IVA's target population is not defined in terms of specific geographical, socioeconomic, or performance-level criteria. Rather, our aim is to serve students and the parents of students
who *value:*

- A small, personalized learning community;
- Small class sizes;
- An educational approach that stresses a felt appreciation and genuine understanding of academic content;

who *believe* that:

- Learning and knowledge are good and that education, properly conducted, should have a *humanizing* effect;

- One of the greatest things an education can provide is a genuine "love of learning" and an ability to think deeply, carefully, and well;

- Education, properly conducted, is personally transformative, affecting many of one's most fundamental beliefs, attitudes, values, and skills;

who are *open* to:

- Becoming curious, wondering, reflecting, asking questions, and thinking for themselves;

- Engaging their education *actively* and *intentionally*;

- *Enjoying* knowledge and learning for their own sake;

- Having their intellectual character stretched and molded by their education.

Given its unique focus, IVA is especially well positioned to embrace the rich diversity of the student population in Long Beach. IVA's instructional vision speaks to the *humanity* of its subjects. As such, it is likely to appeal to students and parents in ways that are independent of their more particular identities and backgrounds. We do not expect students and parents will already be familiar with an intellectual virtues educational model, much less that they will already possess the dispositions in question. Rather, our expectation is that students and parents who are exposed to the model at information sessions or through other outreach channels will find the model compelling and be motivated to apply.

While emphasizing the humanities, other liberal arts and sciences, and academic rigor, IVA's vision is far from *elitist*. To illustrate, we note that students who might do reasonably well in exclusive or elitist educational settings could fail to flourish at IVA. A student with a very high IQ or with a capacious memory, for instance, might nevertheless lack curiosity or inquisitiveness—indeed, might be intellectually unreflective, narrow-minded, or intellectually arrogant—and thus be unlikely to feel comfortable or do very well at IVA. Similarly, the ethos of many exclusive or privileged schools is marked by extreme academic competition and an overriding concern with grades and other external markers. There is, however, significant tension between an ethos of this sort and the spirit of an intellectual virtues approach. The latter prizes intellectual humility, curiosity, and a genuine love of learning—a love that overrides concerns with status and other forms of external recognition. Finally, we note that a student who might struggle in many elite educational settings might do quite well at IVA. For instance, a student of mediocre intelligence (understood in the traditional sense), or with a weak ability for memorization or rapid recall, might nevertheless be very reflective, curious, intellectually careful, and intellectually thorough. In many academic settings, such a student would be unlikely to flourish. At IVA, however, the unique needs of students like this will be known and attended to by their teachers, they will be given the tools and strategies they need to maximize their intellectual potential, and their curiosity, reflectiveness, and other intellectual virtues will be nurtured and rewarded. IVA will be an ideal setting in which to "hook" such students, thereby creating an environment in which they are far more likely to master skills and habits important for success in more traditional academic environments.

IVA will be a diverse and inclusive environment that welcomes, supports, and nurtures students from a wide range of backgrounds and with a range of different gifts and abilities. The common commitment among our students and their parents will be to understanding and practicing those personal qualities or intellectual virtues that are essential to being a true "lover of learning" or "lifelong learner."

NOTES

Introduction

[1]There is some question, especially among Catholics, about whether Luther's famous speech included the last three sentences. However, it is common to attribute these lines to Luther as evidenced by their use in work by the respected Catholic apologist Peter Kreeft. See, for instance, Kreeft, "Justification by Faith," in *Fundamentals of the Faith* (San Francisco: Ignatius Press, 1988), pp. 277-81. Posted on Catholic Education Resource Center, http://catholiceducation.org/articles/apologetics/apoo27.html.

[2]Owen Gingerich, *The Eye of Heaven: Ptolemy, Copernicus, Kepler* (New York: American Institute of Physics, 1993), pp. 39-51.

[3]William Hague, *William Wilberforce: The Life of the Great Anti-slave Trade Campaigner* (London: HarperPress, 2007), pp. xv-xviii, 503.

[4]"Poll: U.S. Teens Say Cheating Widespread," analysis by Dalia Sussman, *ABC Primetime*, April 29, 2004, http://abcnews.go.com/Primetime/story?id=131890 &page=1. Michael J. Weiss ("High-Wired Cheating: Special Teens and School Report," *Family Circle*, April 1, 2007, pp. 46ff., familycircle.com; see also www.thefreelibrary.com/Cheating+article+prompts+PR+effort.-a0160901663) cites a study by Duke and Rutgers university professors of 18,000 American high school students that shows 66 percent of students admitted to cheating. Regarding marital infidelity, the statistics are notoriously erratic, likely because of the shame and secrecy associated with affairs. Some researchers such as Tony DeLorenzo and Dawn Ricci of All State Investigators claim that 60 percent of marriages suffer from infidelity (*Warning Signs: How to Know if Your Partner is Cheating, and What to Do About it* [The Lyons Press, 2009], back cover). However, the Kinsey Institute claims that only between 30 and 40 percent (approximately) of marriages experience infidelity (www.kinseyinstitute.org /resources/FAQ.html#infidelity).

[5]Jason Bachr, *The Inquiring Mind. On Intellectual Virtues and Virtue Epistemology* (Oxford: Oxford University Press, 2011); Robert C. Roberts and W. Jay Wood, *Intellectual Virtues: An Essay in Regulative Epistemology* (Oxford: Clarendon, 2007).

[6]Portions of the following several chapters were published by the author as "Intellectual Character: The Missing Core of Christian Education," *Christian School*

Education, November 2011, pp. 22-25.
[7]Paraphrase of Romans 12:2.

Chapter 1: Intellectual Courage

[1]C. S. Lewis, *The Screwtape Letters* (Oxford: Isis Large Print Books, 1990), p. 117.
[2]Stephen Jay Gould, *Leonardo's Mountain of Clams and the Diet of Worms: Essays on Natural History* (London: Jonathan Cape Ltd., 1998), pp. 251-65.
[3]For a very critical look at Luther and the results of the Reformation, see the account of the scientist Stephen Jay Gould, *Leonardo's Mountain of Clams and the Diet of Worms,* pp. 251-65. For evidence of the material, cultural and scientific achievements unleashed by the Reformation, see David S. Landes, *The Wealth and Poverty of Nations: Why Some Are So Rich and Some So Poor* (New York: Norton, 1998); Max Weber, *The Protestant Ethic and the "Spirit" of Capitalism,* edited and translated by Peter Baehr and Gordon C. Wells (New York: Penguin, 2002); and Robert K. Merton, *Science, Technology, and Society in Seventeenth-century England* (New York: Fertig, 2001).
[4]Widely attributed to H. L. Mencken.

Chapter 2: Intellectual Carefulness

[1]"For Want of Hyphen Venus Rocket Is Lost," *New York Times,* July 28, 1962.
[2]William James, from "The Will to Believe," first published in *The New World* 5 (1896): pp. 327-47.
[3]Aristotle, *Nicomachean Ethics,* trans. W. D. Ross, rev. J. O. Urmson and J. L. Ackrill (Oxford: Oxford University Press, 1998), p. 3.
[4]"Media Talk; Error in Quote Stirs Arguments over Adams Legacy," *New York Times,* July 23, 2001.
[5]Alexander Solzhenitsyn, address at Harvard Class Day Afternoon Exercises, June 8, 1978, www.columbia.edu/cu/augustine/arch/solzhenitsyn/harvard1978.html.
[6]Liz Halloran, "Duke's Trial by Media: Why the Seamy Lacrosse Scandal May Be Too Hot to Be True," *U.S. News and World Report,* August 6, 2006, www.usnews.com/usnews/news/articles/060806/14duke_print.htm. This article details the accusations made in *Rolling Stone,* the *Los Angeles Times* and others.

Chapter 3: Intellectual Tenacity

[1]Neil Postman, *Amusing Ourselves to Death: Public Discourse in the Age of Show Business* (New York: Viking, 1985), p. 80; Allan Bloom, *The Closing of the American Mind: How Higher Education Has Failed Democracy and Impoverished the Souls of Today's Students* (New York: Simon & Schuster, 1987), p. 59; William J. Bennett, "Quantifying America's Decline," *Wall Street Journal,* March 15, 1993.
[2]Quoted in "Thomas Edison," *Harper's Monthly,* September 1932.
[3]Thomas Paine, "The Crisis No. I," *The American Crisis* (a series of tracts concerning the American Revolution), December 23, 1776.

Chapter 4: Intellectual Fair-mindedness

[1]Allan Bloom, *The Closing of the American Mind: How Higher Education Has*

Failed Democracy and Impoverished the Souls of Today's Students (New York: Simon & Schuster, 1987), p. 25.

²G. K. Chesterton, *Orthodoxy* (New York: Doubleday, 1990), p. 33.

³Story recounted in Alister McGrath, *A Passion for Truth: The Intellectual Coherence of Evangelicalism* (Downers Grove, IL: InterVarsity Press, 1996), pp. 190-91.

⁴C. S. Lewis, *The Abolition of Man* (London: G. Bles, 1946), p. 21.

⁵Giovanni Pico della Mirandola, *Oration on the Dignity of Man*, trans. A. Robert Gaponigri (Washington, DC: Regnery Publishing, 1996), pp. xi-xiii.

⁶Ibid., p. 41.

⁷Owen Gingerich, *The Eye of Heaven: Ptolemy, Copernicus, Kepler* (New York: American Institute of Physics, 1993), especially pp. 39-51.

⁸A. N. Whitehead, *Science and the Modern World* (New York: Mentor Book, 1948), p. 49.

Chapter 5: Intellectual Curiosity

¹Paul Brand and Philip Yancey, *Pain: The Gift Nobody Wants* (London: HarperCollins, 1994).

²Michael Guillen, *Five Equations That Changed the World: The Power and Poetry of Mathematics* (New York: Hyperion, 1995), p. 23.

³Dr. Tom Bulick, vice president of Student Affairs, Trinity Western University, circa 1990.

⁴Stephanie Simon, "The United States of Mind," *Wall Street Journal*, September 23, 2008.

Chapter 6: Intellectual Honesty

¹Erika Cohen, letter to the editor, "Betrayal of Trust: The Jayson Blair Scandal," *New York Times*, May 13, 2003; Rem Rieder, "The Jayson Blair Affair," *American Journalism Review*, June 2003, http://ajr.org/article.asp?id=3019; "Corrections to Articles by Jayson Blair," *New York Times*, June 11, 2003. See also Blair's book on the scandal, *Burning Down My Master's House: My Life at the New York Times* (Beverly Hills, CA: New Millennium Press, 2004), in which he claims his journalistic sins were at least partially caused by mental illness.

²Eight years later, in an attempt to recover his reputation, Dan Rather wrote *Rather Outspoken: My Life in the News* (New York: Grand Central, 2012), in which he claimed that the main point of the story was correct. While this claim remains highly controversial, the fact that CBS News engaged in unethical journalism throughout the episode is not. See the 234-page report on CBS's internal investigation by Dick Thornburgh and Louis D. Boccardi, *Report of the Independent Review Panel*, CBS News, January 5, 2005, pp. 14-16, www.cbsnews.com/htdocs/pdf/complete_report/CBS_Report.pdf.

³"Disgraced Korean Cloning Scientist Indicted," *New York Times*, May 12, 2006.

⁴Alexander Solzhenitsyn, address at Harvard Class Day Afternoon Exercises, June 8, 1978, www.columbia.edu/cu/augustine/arch/solzhenitsyn/harvard1978.html.

[5]Study cited in Michael J. Weiss, "High-wired Cheating: Special Teens and School Report," *Family Circle*, April 1, 2007, pp. 49-50.

[6]Nancy Shulins, "N.Y. Weatherman: Sun Is Shining on Bob Harris as Storm Clears," *Los Angeles Times,* May 19, 1985. The quote is attributed to an article by Nancy Shulins, in the *Journal News,* Nyack, New York.

[7]Theodore Roosevelt, "The Man in the Arena: Citizenship in a Republic," address delivered at the Sorbonne, Paris, April 23, 1910, www.conservativeforum.org /EssaysForm.asp?ID=6312.

[8]Dallas Willard, *The Divine Conspiracy: Rediscovering Our Hidden Life in God* (San Francisco: HarperSanFrancisco, 1998), p. 343.

[9]Quoted in Covey, *Seven Habits of Highly Effective People*, p. 305.

[10]"Science: End as a Man," *Time*, November 30, 1953.

[11]Dallas Willard, in Phillip E. Johnson, *The Wedge of Truth* (Downers Grove, IL: InterVarsity Press, 2000), p. 9.

Chapter 7: Intellectual Humility

[1]C. S. Lewis, *The Screwtape Letters* (Oxford: Isis Large Print Books, 1990), p. 117.

[2]G. K. Chesterton, *Orthodoxy* (New York: Doubleday, 1990), p. 32.

[3]Czesław Miłosz, *The Captive Mind,* trans. Jane Zielonko (New York: Knopf, 1953), p. 3.

[4]The story and the quote come from Carl Sandburg, *Abraham Lincoln: The Prairie Years and the War Years* (1970; New York: Mariner, 2002), p. 354.

[5]It is one of history's cruel ironies that while some in the French aristocracy did embody this attitude, Marie Antoinette (the person incorrectly assigned responsibility for this statement) appears to have been both aware of the peasants' situation and highly sympathetic. Antonia Fraser, *Marie Antoinette: The Journey* (New York: Anchor, 2002), p. 135.

[6]C. S. Lewis, *Mere Christianity* (London: Harper Collins, 2001), p. 122.

[7]Lewis, *Screwtape Letters,* p. 55.

Part 2: The Fruits of Intellectual Character

[1]C. S. Lewis, *Mere Christianity* (London: HarperCollins, 2001), p. 32.

Chapter 8: The Benefits of Knowing More About More

[1]Jack Flam, "A Convergence of Faith and Reason," *Wall Street Journal*, February 18, 2012, http://online.wsj.com/article/SB10001424052970204136404577211450920419794.html.

[2]Steve Connor, "The Core of Truth Behind Sir Isaac Newton's Apple," *The Independent,* January 18, 2010, www.independent.co.uk/news/science/the-core-of-truth-behind-sir-isaac-newtons-apple-1870915.html.

Chapter 9: The Benefits of Better Thinking

[1]Andrew Hussey, "ZZ Top," *The Observer,* April 4, 2004, www.guardian.co.uk/football/2004/apr/04/sport.features.

[2]This story is an adaptation of a traditional folktale included in William Bennett,

ed., *The Moral Compass: Stories for a Life's Journey* (New York: Simon & Schuster, 1995), pp. 193-95.

Chapter 10: Loving God
[1]Thomas Aquinas, "Whether There Is Love of Choice in the Angels?" *Summa Theologica*, objection 2, www.ccel.org/ccel/aquinas/summa.FP_Q60_A2.html.
[2]C. S. Lewis, *Mere Christianity* (London: HarperCollins, 2001), p. 78.
[3]Andreas J. Köstenberger, *Excellence: The Character of God and the Pursuit of Scholarly Virtue* (Wheaton, IL: Crossway, 2011), p. 46.

Chapter 11: Loving Your Neighbor
[1]J. P. Moreland, *Love Your God with All Your Mind* (Colorado Springs: NavPress, 1997), p. 74.
[2]Max Weber, *The Protestant Ethic and the "Spirit" of Capitalism*, ed. and trans. Peter Baehr and Gordon C. Wells (New York: Penguin, 2002).
[3]Robert K. Merton, *Science, Technology & Society in Seventeenth-Century England* (New York: Fertig, 2001).
[4]David Landes, "Culture Makes Almost All the Difference," pp. 2-13; Seymour Martin Lipset and Gabriel Salman Lenz, "Corruption, Culture, and Markets," pp. 112-25; Ronald Inglehart, "Culture and Democracy," pp. 80-97; Francis Fukuyama, "Social Capital," pp. 98-111; all in *Culture Matters: How Values Shape Human Progress*, ed. Lawrence E. Harrison and Samuel P. Huntington (New York: Basic, 2000).
[5]John Karanja, "Evangelical Attitudes Toward Democracy in Kenya," in *Evangelical Christianity and Democracy in Africa*, ed. Terence O. Ranger (Oxford: Oxford University Press, 2008), pp. 67-93; Nixon Kavai, "Lawyer Paul Muite and Rev. Mutava Musyimi's Belated Entry into Kenya's 2012 Presidential Race Raise [*sic*] Eyebrows," *The Weekly Vision*, October 26, 2011, www.theweeklyvision.blogspot.co.uk/2011/10/lawyer-paul-muite-and-rev-mutava.html?m=1.
[6]Václav Havel et al., *The Power of the Powerless: Citizens Against the State in Central-eastern Europe*, ed. John Keane (New York: Palach Press, 1985), pp. 27-40.

Chapter 12: Developing Virtuous Intellectual Character
[1]Dallas Willard, *The Divine Conspiracy: Rediscovering Our Hidden Life in God* (San Francisco: HarperSanFrancisco, 1998), p. 324.
[2]*A Prairie Home Companion with Garrison Keillor*, prairiehome.publicradio.org.
[3]See appendix C.
[4]Dallas Willard, *Renovation of the Heart: Putting on the Character of Christ* (Colorado Springs: NavPress, 2002), pp. 83-84.
[5]C. S. Lewis, *Mere Christianity* (London: HarperCollins, 2001), p. 188.
[6]William James, *Habit* (New York: Henry Holt & Co., 1890), p. 60; italics mine.
[7]Ibid.

Chapter 13: Seven Suggestions for Educators and Parents

[1]Stephen R. Covey, *The Seven Habits of Highly Effective People: Restoring the Character Ethic* (New York: Simon & Schuster, 1989), p. 137.

[2]See appendix A.

[3]Covey, *Seven Habits*, p. 134.

[4]This example is courtesy of my good friend Dr. Chris Anderson of The Perse School, Cambridge, and Eden Baptist Church, Cambridge.

[5]The Sapir-Whorf hypothesis is outlined in Ron Ritchhart, *Intellectual Character: What It Is, Why It Matters, and How to Get It* (San Francisco: Wiley & Sons, 2002), pp. 116-17. It should also be noted that, while the basic principle of the hypothesis is largely accepted (that our vocabulary does influence our ability to conceptualize), researchers have widely dismissed the ability of language to determine our thinking. In other words, the soft version of the hypothesis is accepted, but the more extreme representations of the hypothesis have not been.

[6]See Jason S. Baehr, *The Inquiring Mind: On Intellectual Virtues and Virtue Epistemology* (Oxford: Oxford University Press, 2011).

[7]For a good summary of Francis Bacon's contribution to what we now call the scientific method, see Juergen Klein, "Francis Bacon," *Stanford Encyclopedia of Philosophy*, December 29, 2003, http://plato.stanford.edu/entries/francis-bacon/.

[8]For an excellent discussion of the role of feelings in our lives and the need to engage our minds in the evaluation of those feelings, see Dallas Willard, *Renovation of the Heart: Putting on the Character of Christ* (Colorado Springs: NavPress, 2002), pp. 122-38.

[9]For additional information on a number of excellent thinking routines, see Ritchhart, *Intellectual Character*, pp. 85-111. This is also where I first came across the phrase *thinking routine*.

[10]A further explanation of this common thinking routine is found in Ritchhart, *Intellectual Character*, pp. 85-111.

[11]"DoD News Briefing—Secretary Rumsfeld and Gen. Myers," U.S. Department of Defense News Transcript, February 12, 2002, www.defense.gov/Transcripts/Transcript.aspx?TranscriptID=2636.

[12]Neil J. Anderson, "The Role of Metacognition in Second Language Teaching and Learning," Center for Applied Linguistics, EDO-FL-01-10, April 2002, www.cal.org/resources/digest/0110anderson.html.

Conclusion

[1]Keith Green, "The Sheep and the Goats," *The Keith Green Collection*, sound recording, released August 11, 1981.

[2]To my knowledge no one has successfully proved that Goethe made this remark, although it remains widely attributed to him.

[3]Quoted in Stephen R. Covey, *The Seven Habits of Highly Effective People: Restoring the Character Ethic* (New York: Simon & Schuster, 1989), p. 297.

References

Ablard, Karen, and Rachelle E. Lipschultz. 1998. "Self-Regulated Learning in High-Achieving Students: Relations to Advanced Reasoning, Achievement Goals, and Gender." *Journal of Educational Psychology* 90: 94-101.

Andrews, Jane, and Helen Higson. 2008. "Graduate Employability, 'Soft Skills' Versus 'Hard' Business Knowledge." *Higher Education in Europe* 33 (4): 411-22.

Angelo, Thomas. 1995. "Classroom Assessment for Critical Thinking." *Teaching of Psychology* 22: 6-7.

Baehr, Jason. 2011a. *The Inquiring Mind: On Intellectual Virtues and Virtue Epistemology.* Oxford: Oxford University Press.

———. 2011b. "The Structure of Open-Mindedness." *Canadian Journal of Philosophy* 41 (2): 191-213.

Baron, Jonathan. 1981. "Reflective Thinking as a Goal of Education." *Intelligence* 5 (4): 291-309.

Benninga, Jacques, Marvin Berkowitz, Phyllis Kuehn and Karen Smith. 2003. "The Relationship of Character Education Implementation and Academic Achievement in Elementary Schools." *Journal of Research in Character Education* 1 (1): 19-32.

Berkowitz, Marvin, Victor Battistich and Melinda Bier. 2008. "What Works in Character Education: What Is Known and What Needs to Be Known." In *Handbook of Moral and Character Education,* edited by D. Narvaez and L. P. Nucci: 414-31. New York: Routledge.

Berkowitz, Marvin, and Melinda Bier. 2004. "Research-Based Character Education." *Annals of the American Academy of Political and Social Science* 591: 72-85.

———. 2006. "What Works in Character Education: A Research-Driven Guide for Educators." Character Education Partnership. www.characterandcitizenship .org.

———. 2007. "What Works in Character Education." *Journal of Research in Character Education* 5 (1): 29-48.

Bers, Trudy, Marilee McGowan and Alan Rubin. 1996. "The Disposition to Think Critically Among Community College Students: The California Critical Thinking Dispositions Inventory." *The Journal of General Education* 45: 197-223.

Beyer, Barry. 1987. *Practical Strategies for the Teaching of Thinking*. Boston: Allyn & Bacon.

Brooks, David, and Frank G. Goble. 1997. *The Case for Character Education: The Role of the School in Teaching Values and Virtues*. Northridge, CA: Studio 4 Productions.

Carr, David. 2007. "Character in Teaching." *British Journal of Educational Studies* 55 (4): 369-89.

Cornoldi, Cesare. 2010. "Metacognition, Intelligence, and Academic Performance." In *Metacognition, Strategy Use, and Instruction*, edited by Harriet Salatas Waters and Wolfgang Schneider: 257-80. New York: The Guilford Press.

Costa, A. 1989. *Techniques for Teaching Thinking*. Seaside, CA: Critical Thinking Press.

Coutinho, S. 2008. "Self-Efficacy, Metacognition, and Performance." *North American Journal of Psychology* 10: 166.

Craft, Anna, Howard Gardner and Guy Claxton, eds. 2008. *Creativity, Wisdom, and Trusteeship*. Thousand Oaks, CA: Corwin Press.

Craig, Cheryl, and Louise Deretchin, eds. 2010. *Cultivating Curious and Creative Minds*. Lanham, MD: Rowman & Littlefield.

Curren, Randall. 2001. "Moral Education." In *The Encyclopedia of Ethics*, 2nd ed., edited by Lawrence and Charlotte Becker: 1127-31.

Davidson, Matthew, Vladimir Khmelkov and Thomas Lickona. 2010. "The Power of Character: Needed for, and Developed from, Teaching and Learning." In *International Research Handbook on Values Education and Student Well-Being*, edited by Terence Lovat, Ron Toomey and Neville Clement, Part 2: 427-54. New York: Springer.

Deemer, S. 2004. "Classroom Goal Orientation in High School Classrooms: Revealing Links Between Teacher Beliefs and Classroom Environments." *Educational Research* 46: 73-90.

DeRoche, Edward F., and Mary M. Williams. 1998. *Educating Hearts and Minds: A Comprehensive Character Education Framework*. Thousand Oaks, CA: Corwin Press.

Dewey, John. 1902. *The Child and the Curriculum*. Chicago: University of Chicago Press.

———. (1910) 1997. *How We Think*. Reprint, Mineola, NY: Dover.

Elkind, D. H. 1997. "The Socratic Approach to Character Education." *Educational Leadership* 54 (8): 56-59.

Ennis, Robert. 1993. "Critical Thinking Assessment." *Theory into Practice* 32 (2): 179-86.

Facione, P. A., et al. 2000. "The Disposition Toward Critical Thinking: Its Character, Measurement to Critical Thinking Skills." *Journal of Informal Logic* 20 (1): 61-84.

Goldie, Peter. 2012. "Loss of Affect in Intellectual Activity." *Emotion Review* 4 (2): 122-26.

Greene, Barbara, et al. 2004. "Predicting High School Students' Cognitive Engagement and Achievement: Contributions of Classroom Perceptions and Motivations." *Contemporary Educational Psychology* 29: 462-82.

Gullatt, David. 2008. "Enhancing Student Learning Through Arts Integration: Implications for the Profession." *High School Journal* 91 (4): 12-25.

Halpern, Diane. 1997. *Critical Thinking Across the Curriculum: A Brief Edition of Thought and Knowledge.* New York: Erlbaum.

Hare, William. 1983. *Open-Mindedness and Education.* Montreal: McGill-Queens University Press.

———. 1985a. *In Defence of Open-Mindedness.* Montreal: McGill-Queens University Press.

———. 1985b. "Open-Mindedness in the Classroom." *Journal of the Philosophy of Education* 19: 251-59.

———. 1993. *What Makes a Good Teacher.* London, Ontario: Althouse Press.

———. 1995. *Teaching and the Socratic Virtues.* St. John's, Newfoundland: Memorial University Press.

———. 2003. "Is It Good to Be Open-Minded?" *International Journal of Applied Philosophy* 17 (1): 73-87.

Haynes, C., et al. 1997. "Fostering Civic Virtue: Character Education in the Social Studies." *Social Education* 61: 225-27.

Hoge, J. D. 2002. "Character Education, Citizenship Education, and the Social Studies." *Social Studies* 93 (3): 103-8.

Holland, Daniel. 2004. "Integrating Mindfulness Meditation and Somatic Awareness into a Public Educational Setting." *Journal of Humanistic Psychology* 44 (4): 468-84.

Huebner, Dwayne. 1995. "Education and Spirituality." *JCT: An Interdisciplinary Journal of Curriculum Studes* 11 (2): 13-34.

Hughes, Jill Elaine. 2011. "21st Century Skills: Critical Thinking." http://www.phoenix.edu/forward/careers/2011/08/21st-century-skills-critical-thinking.html.

Hurley, Casey. 2009. *The Six Virtues of the Educated Person.* Lanham, MD: Rowman & Littlefield.

Hyland, Terry. 2009. "Mindfulness and the Therapeutic Function of Education." *Journal of the Philosophy of Education* 43 (1): 119-31.

Jackson, Philip W., Robert E. Boostrom and David T. Hansen. 1993. *The Moral Life of Schools.* San Francisco: Jossey-Bass.

Kalantzis, Mary, and Bill Cope. 2005. *Learning by Design.* Melbourne: Common Ground.

Kapusnick, Regina, and Christine Hauslein. 2001. "The 'Silver Cup' of Differentiated Instruction." *Kappa Delta Pi Record* 37 (4): 156-59.

Keil, Frank. 2006. "Explanation and Understanding." *Annual Review of Psychology* 57: 227-54.

Kirby, Erika, et al. 2006. "The Jesuit Difference: Narratives of Negotiating Spiritual Values and Secular Practices." *Communication Studies* 57 (1): 87-105.

Kitchener, Karen Strohm. 1983. "Educational Goals and Reflective Thinking." *The Educational Forum* 48 (1): 74-95.

Klitz, Gary. 2003. "An Integrated Approach to Character-Education in an Alternative High School." *Current Issues in Education* 6: 18.

Kohlberg, Lawrence. 1981–1984. *Essays on Moral Development: The Philosophy of Moral Development.* 2 vols. San Francisco: Harper and Row.

Kohn, A. 1997. "How Not to Teach Values: A Critical Look at Character Education." *Phi Delta Kappan* 78: 429-39.

Land, Susan, and Barbara Greene. 2000. "Project-Based Learning with the World Wide Web: A Qualitative Study of Resource Integration." *Educational Technology Research and Development* 48 (1): 45-66.

Langer, Ellen. 1990. *Mindfulness.* Boston: De Capo Books.

———. 1993. "A Mindful Education." *Educational Psychologist* 28 (1): 43-50.

Lee, Hea-Jin. 2005. "Understanding and Assessing Preservice Teachers' Reflective Thinking." *Teaching and Teacher Education* 21 (6): 699-715.

Leming, James S. 1993. *Character Education: Lessons From the Past, Models for the Future.* Camden, ME: The Institute for Global Ethics.

Lickona, Thomas. 1992. *Educating for Character: How Our Schools Can Teach Respect and Responsibility.* New York: Bantam.

———. 1993. "The Return of Character Education." *Educational Leadership* 51 (3): 6-11.

Lickona, Thomas, and Matthew Davidson. 2005. *Smart and Good High Schools: Integrating Excellence and Ethics for Success in School, Work, and Beyond.* Washington, DC: Character Education Partnership.

Livingston, Jennifer. 1997. "Metacognition." www.gse.buffalo.edu/fas/shuell/cep564/Metacog.htm.

Lucangeli, D., C. Cornoldi and M. Tellarini. 1998. "Metacognition and Learning Disabilities in Mathematics." In *Advances In Learning and Behavioral Disabilities,* edited by T. E. Scruggs and M. A. Mastropieri: 219-44. Greenwich, CT: JAI.

Milson, A. J. 2000. "Creating a Curriculum for Character Development: A Case Study." *The Clearing House* 74 (2): 89-94.

Mishook, Jacob, and Mindy Kornhaber. 2006. "Arts Integration in an Era of Accountability." *Arts Education Policy Review* 107 (4): 3-11.

Molnar, Alex, ed. 1997. *The Construction of Children's Character: The Ninety-sixth Yearbook of the National Society for the Study of Education.* Chicago: University of Chicago Press.

Moore, Lori, and Rick Rudd. 2002. "Using Socratic Questioning in the Classroom." *Agricultural Education Magazine* 75 (3): 24-25.

Murname, Richard, and Frank Levy. 1996. *Teaching the New Basic Skills: Principles for Educating Children to Thrive in a Changing Economy.* New York: Free Press.

Norris, Stephen. 1985. "Synthesis of Research on Critical Thinking." *Educational Leadership* (May): 40-45.

Null, J. W., and A. J. Milson. 2003. "Beyond Marquee Morality: Virtue in the Social Studies." *The Social Studies* (May/June): 119-22.

Nussbaum, Martha. 2010. *Not for Profit.* Princeton, NJ: Princeton University Press.

Paul, Richard. 1985. "Critical Thinking Research." *Educational Leadership* (May): 46-47.

———. 2004. "The State of Critical Thinking Today: The Need for a Substantive Concept of Critical Thinking." The Critical Thinking Community. www.criti calthinking.org/resources/articles/the-state-ct-today.shtml.

Paul, Richard, and Linda Elder. 2008. "Critical Thinking: The Art of Socratic Questioning, Part III." *Journal of Developmental Education* 31 (3): 34-35.

Perkins, David. 1993. "Teaching for Understanding." *American Educator* 17 (3): 28-35.

———. 2008. *Making Learning Whole.* San Francisco: Jossey-Bass.

Perkins, David, Eileen Jay and Shari Tishman. 1993. "New Conceptions of Thinking: From Ontology to Education." *Educational Psychologist* 28 (1): 67-85.

———. 1994. "Assessing Thinking: A Framework for Measuring Critical Thinking and Problem Solving at the College Level." In *The National Assessment of College Student Learning: Identification of the Skills to Be Taught, Learned, and Assessed,* edited by A. Greenwood: 65-112. Washington, DC: The US Government Printing Office.

Perkins, David, and Ron Ritchhart. 2004. "When Is Good Thinking?" In *Motivation, Emotion, and Cognition,* edited by David Yun Dai and Robert Sternberg: 351-84. New York: Erlbaum and Associates.

Perkins, David, Shari Tishman, Ron Ritchhart, Kiki Donis and Al Andrade. 2000. "Intelligence in the Wild: A Dispositional View of Intellectual Traits." *Educational Psychology Review* 12 (3): 269-93.

Phillips, V. 1995. *Helping Your At-Risk Students Develop Greater Motivation, Responsibility, and Self-Discipline (Grades 6-12).* Bellevue: Bureau of Education and Research.

Piaget, Jean. 1965. *The Moral Judgment of the Child.* New York: The Free Press.

Richards, Mary Caroline. 1980. "The Public School and the Education of the Whole Person." *Teachers College Record* 82 (1): 47-75.

Ritchhart, Ron. 2001. "From IQ to IC: A Dispositional View of Intelligence." *Roeper Review* 23 (3): 143-50.

———. 2002. *Intellectual Character: What It Is, Why It Matters, and How to Get It.* San Francisco: Jossey-Bass.

———. 2007. "The Seven R's of a Quality Curriculum." *Education Quarterly Australia.* http://www.equa.edu.au.

Ritchhart, Ron, Mark Church and Karin Morrison. 2011. *Making Thinking Visible: How to Promote Engagement, Understanding, and Independence for All Learners.* San Francisco: Jossey-Bass.

Ritchhart, Ron, Patricia Palmer, Mark Church and Shari Tishman. 2006. "Thinking Routines: Establishing Patterns of Thinking in the Classroom." Paper presented at the annual meeting of the American Educational Research Association, San Francisco, April.

Ritchhart, Ron, and David Perkins. 2000. "Life in the Mindful Classroom: Nurturing the Disposition of Mindfulness." *Journal of Social Issues* 56 (1): 27-47.

———. 2008. "Making Thinking Visible." *Educational Leadership* 65 (5): 57-61.

Ritchhart, Ron, Terri Turner and Linor Hadar. 2009. "Uncovering Students' Thinking About Thinking Using Concept Maps." *Metacognition Learning* 4 (2): 145-59.

Roberts, Robert, and Jay Wood. 2007. *Intellectual Virtues: An Essay in Regulative Epistemology*. Oxford: Oxford University Press.

Rodgers, Carol. 2002. "Defining Reflection: Another Look at John Dewey and Reflective Thinking." *Teachers College Record* 104 (4): 842-66.

Scheffler, Israel. 1991. *In Praise of Cognitive Emotions*. New York: Routledge.

Schonert-Reichl, Kimberly, and Molly Stewart Lawlor. 2010. "The Effects of a Mindfulness-Based Education Program on Pre- and Early Adolescents' Well-Being and Social and Emotional Competence." *Mindfulness* 1 (3): 137-51.

Schulz, Bernd. 2008. "The Importance of Soft Skills: Education Beyond Academic Knowledge." *Journal of Language and Communication* (June): 146-54.

Scriven, Michael, and Richard, Paul. 1987. "Critical Thinking as Defined by the National Council for Excellence in Critical Thinking." Paper presented at the Eighth Annual International Conference on Critical Thinking and Education Reform.

Seidel, Steve, Shari Tishman, Ellen Winner, Lois Hetland and Patricia Palmer. 2009. *Qualities of Quality: Excellence in Arts Education and How to Achieve It*. Report commissioned by the Wallace Foundation. Project Zero, Harvard Graduate School of Education.

Seligman, Martin, and Mihaly Csikszentmihalyi. 2000. "Positive Psychology: An Introduction." *American Psychologist* 55 (1): 5-14.

Seligman, Martin, Randall Ernst, Jane Gillham, Karen Reivich and Mark Linkins. 2009. "Positive Education: Positive Psychology and Classroom Interventions." *Oxford Review of Education* 35 (3): 293-311.

Siegel, Harvey. 1980. "Critical Thinking as an Educational Ideal." *The Educational Forum* 45 (1): 7-23.

———. 1988. *Educating Reason: Rationality, Critical Thinking, and Education*. New York: Routledge.

———. 2002. "Critical Thinking." In *The Blackwell Guide to the Philosophy of Education*, edited by Nigel Blake, Paul Smeyers, Richard D. Smith and Paul Standish: 181-93. Oxford: Blackwell.

———. 2004. "High Stakes Testing, Educational Aims and Ideals, and Responsible Assessment." *Theory and Research in Education* 2 (3): 219-33.

Smith, Stephen. 2012. "Ticket to a Better Life." *American Public Media/American*

Radio Works. http://americanradioworks.publicradio.org/index.html.

Snyder, Frank, Brian Flay, Samuel Vuchinich, Alan Accock, Isaac Washburn, Michael Beets and Kin-Kit Li. 1980. "Critical Thinking as an Educational Ideal." *The Educational Forum* 45 (1): 7-23.

————. 2010. "Impact of a Social-Emotional and Character Development Program on School-Level Indicators of Academic Achievement, Absenteeism, and Disciplinary Outcomes: A Matched-Pair, Cluster Randomized, Controlled Trial." *Journal of Research on Educational Effectiveness* 3 (1): 26-55.

Sperling, R., B. Howard, R. Staley and N. DuBois. 2004. "Metacognition and Self-Regulated Learning Constructs." *Educational Research and Evaluation* 10: 132.

Spiecker, Ben, and Jan Steutel. 1995. "Political Liberalism, Civic Education, and the Dutch Government." *Journal of Moral Education* 24 (1): 383-94.

Starratt, Robert. 1994. *Building an Ethical School.* New York: Routledge.

Sternberg, Robert. 1986. *Critical Thinking: Its Nature, Measurement, and Improvement.* Washington, DC: National Institute of Education.

————. 2003. *Wisdom, Intelligence, and Creativity Synthesized.* Cambridge: Cambridge University Press.

Steutel, J. W. 2002. "The Virtue Approach to Moral Education: Some Conceptual Clarification." *Journal of the Philosophy of Education* 31 (3): 395-407.

Thomas, John W. 2000. *A Review of Research on Project Based Learning.* San Rafael, CA: The Autodesk Foundation.

Tishman, Shari, and Patricia Palmer. 2005. "Visible Thinking." *Leadership Compass* 2 (4): 1-3.

Tishman, Shari, David Perkins and Eileen Jay. 1993. "Teaching Thinking Dispositions: From Transmission to Enculturation." *Theory into Practice* 32 (3): 147-53.

————. 1995. *The Thinking Classroom: Teaching and Learning in a Culture of Thinking.* Needham, MA: Allyn & Bacon.

Tomlinson, C. A., and Jay McTighe. 2006. *Integrating Differentiated Instruction and Understanding by Design.* Danvers, MA: ASCD.

Tsui, Lisa. 1999. "Courses and Instruction Affecting Critical Thinking." *Research in Higher Education* 40: 185-200.

————. 2002. "Fostering Critical Thinking Through Effective Pedagogy." *The Journal of Higher Education* 73 (6): 740-63.

Van Gelder, Tim. 2005. "Teaching Critical Thinking: Some Lessons from Cognitive Science." *College Teaching* 53: 41-46.

Vygotsky, L. S. 1978. *Mind in Society.* Cambridge, MA: Harvard University Press.

Waters, Harriet Salatas, and Wolfgang Schneider, eds. 2010. *Metacognition, Strategy Use, and Instruction.* New York: The Guilford Press.

Wiggins, Grant, and Jay McTighe. 2005. *Understanding by Design,* 2nd ed. New Jersey: Prentice Hall.

Winne, Philip. 1995. "Inherent Details in Self-Regulated Learning." *Educational Psychologist* 30 (4): 173-87.

Wiske, Martha, ed. 1998. *Teaching for Understanding: Linking Research with Practice.* San Francisco: Jossey-Bass.

Wolk, Steven. 2008. "Joy in School." *The Positive Classroom* 66 (1): 8-15.

Wolters, C. 1999. "The Relation Between High School Students' Motivational Regulation and Their Use of Learning Strategies, Effort, and Classroom Performance." *Learning and Individual Differences* 11: 281-300.

Yun Dai, David, and Robert Sternberg. 2004. *Motivation, Emotion, and Cognition.* New York: Erlbaum and Associates.

Zagzebski, Linda. 1996. *Virtues of the Mind.* Cambridge: Cambridge University Press.

Subject Index